PERSONAL FINANCE MADE EASY FOR YOUNG ADULTS

DISCOVER HOW TO PAY OFF DEBT FASTER, RAISE YOUR CREDIT SCORE, AND ACHIEVE FINANCIAL FREEDOM BY BUDGETING AND CREATING MULTIPLE INCOME STREAMS

DAKOTA A. MCQUEEN

DEDICATION

This book is dedicated to my cat,

Milo,

with love (and an abundance of wet food at precisely 3:18 am).

—

Actually... hold on, Milo can't read, so if someone

doesn't tell him about this; he may never know.

ฅ(=•ｪ•̀=)

TABLE OF CONTENTS

FREE GIFT, Just for you!

5-Day Money Challenge:
A Guide Toward Financial Literacy and Freedom

* * *

In this challenge, you'll gain access to...

- A simple 5-day challenge to help you achieve financial freedom faster
- Life-changing money facts and myths to expand your knowledge
- A detailed monthly budget to keep you on the right financial track
- A priceless side hustle document to make extra money on the side
- A financial goal sheet to help you meet all your goals
- A financial intelligence mini-book to encourage you to keep learning

Download your FREE copy now!
Visit www.linktr.ee/smartmoneymover
OR scan the QR code with your phone:

PREFACE

Everyone's journey to financial freedom starts somewhere. There's always that one event, person, activity, or something else memorable enough that it becomes your lightbulb moment. Granted, personal finance is a personal affair. No one will stand over your shoulder with a list of demands or targets as you might experience in formal employment settings. All the more reason why when it comes to personal finance, you must always hold yourself accountable.

You learn about money all the time. Everything from how to count it, invest it, convert it to another country's currency, when it's not enough, or when you simply can't get it. While these are important, the most important lesson is how to value money. This has nothing to do with the numbers printed on the notes or engraved on the coin; it's about the role money will play in your life.

Think about it for a moment, from the day you were born, money has been necessary at every step of your life. Your parents needed to clear the hospital bills when you were born, get you into school, keep you warm and safe in a lovely home, feed you, and so on. The list is endless. This is why the best thing you can do today, for your future, is to reevaluate your relationship with money and redefine what money means to you.

Some people learn about money in school or later in their adult lives. My lessons came a little too early in life, but unknown to me at the time, they would lay the foundation for my financial prudence and success in life. You see, money is involved in everything you do in life. Forget about the age-old adage that *"Money is the root of all evil."* These are some of those common misconceptions that give you a distorted perspective on money.

As a first-generation Asian-American, I was raised by parents born into poverty, an experience many people can relate to. Even then, I learned an important lesson from my parents—with drive, desire, and determination, success is never too far away.

MY STORY

My parents had owned my uncle's restaurant by the time I was born. They put in tremendous effort, keeping me in a car seat under the counter while they took care of the restaurant. For context, the restaurant was open 12 hours a day, every day of the week. Running a busy restaurant and raising a baby proved too much to handle. I was kept in a car seat under our restaurant counter because child care was unaffordable. Even though I was born in New York, I was sent to China to live with one of my aunts. I was only three months old!

It would be three and a half years before I set foot back in America. Curtains were falling in the 90s, so video chats or facetime were still unheard of back then. My parents' childhood memories of me at that time were a few pictures of me in cute little outfits taken in China. It would be weeks or months before those could be hand-delivered to them through friends and family members. For three and a half years, all they had of their child were photos and undying faith.

When I eventually got back into the country, I was instantly introduced to the business. I helped around where I could, sweeping the floor, cutting broccoli, stocking sodas, peeling shrimp, folding crab rangoons, and so on. If not for the labor laws, I could probably list these under my work experience, haha!!

I get that this would be classified as child labor or other unsavory terms, but if I look back at how far I've come and where I am today, none of that matters to me. The most important thing for me, in retrospect, was being able to help my parents in their business and learning valuable financial skills from a young age, so I hope Child Protective Services won't be coming after my folks.

Spending most of my childhood in a restaurant was more than an eye-opener. It was a humbling experience. I learned the value of getting the right mindset and work ethic to succeed in life from that tiny restaurant. I learned the incredible power that delayed gratification and sacrificing a few luxuries had for getting out of poverty.

From my childhood to date, I've learned many practical money lessons you'd probably never learn in any class. You see, the academic curriculum primarily teaches us how to handle other people's money. It prepares you to become an amazing accountant, auditor, financial manager, and so on. It teaches you the legalities of money and the potential punishments if you don't do the right thing. For example, when the IRS comes knocking at your door, there's a good chance your days of giving the government a runaround with their money are up. Yes, it might be your hard-earned money, but a fraction of it belongs to the government, so play nice.

One thing they never teach you in school is how to manage your finances. This is why so many excel in their professional financial careers but struggle to get out of crippling debt themselves.

Is money really the root of all evil? The short answer we'll arrive at together by the end of this book is NO!!

Spare a moment, and read about the history of money. Money is something we made up. It started all the way back as precious stones and evolved into the notes, coins, and cryptocurrencies we use today. We created it and use it to mark value in different things: the food you eat, the clothes you wear, the fuel in your car, and so on. Money isn't the root of all evil; it is a resource, an important one, to be precise. Without it, or if you don't have enough of it, your life will probably be quite uncomfortable. With lots of it, you could have an easy life. But then again, if you have lots of it and misuse it, discomfort comes knocking at your door sooner than you know.

This isn't just about you and me; it's also about your friends, neighbors, siblings, and future generations. The lessons you learn today will go a long way in helping you have a better financial future. I've seen people close to me, friends, and colleagues make mistakes so common you probably know someone who did the same thing. I'll share some of these stories throughout the book to highlight some valuable lessons you can take from this book.

Your youth is the perfect time to learn these lessons because this is when most people make life-changing decisions, particularly regarding finances. I wrote this book hoping I can help you rethink your approach to money and, with a new perspective, help you become more proactive at managing personal finances.

INTRODUCTION

Life comes at you fast!

I'm sure you've heard that line before. This phrase is commonly used as an encouragement, or sometimes a warning, to change your ways or risk unsavory consequences in the not-so-distant future. As a young adult, countless activities and choices in your life could warrant such caution. However, let's restrict our discussion to financial well-being.

Up to this point, your parents have probably been accountable for most of your financial needs. In fact, many young adults know nothing more than some basics of *handling* personal finances. I speak of handling instead of managing because management requires discipline that many young adults lack. Don't worry, though. So many adults are in the same boat. The advantage is that you're about to learn to take charge and go from handling to managing your personal finances.

With their parents' backing, many young adults get on smoothly until they graduate from college, and all financial hell breaks loose. You see, as soon as you graduate, and for some people, as soon as they enroll in college, you become accountable for all your financial decisions. You go from receiving a regular allowance or pocket money to planning how to get through the month with the little you have.

This is also the time when you come face-to-face with three issues that will affect your financial future: debt, investment, and financial literacy. These are crucial lessons I often wish I didn't have to learn the hard way, but I did. If you are getting into college, this should be the most exciting time of your life. You're getting into a new world, and I wish you nothing but awesomeness and success. However, it won't be long before you are due for graduation, and the institution sends you on your way with nothing but your certificates and good luck.

I've been through it all. I've been in debt and had terrible credit, so awful that reputable lenders wouldn't even glance at my requests, yet somehow, I kept trying my luck. Like many young adults, I've been in a situation where I didn't understand the difference between debit and credit. I didn't know how loans work, the penalties for missing payments, and so on. I didn't see the difference between wants and needs, assets and liabilities.

I made some ridiculous financial decisions at the time, which today I can afford to laugh about, mainly because I am in a better place financially. As I write this book, I consistently invest 20% of my monthly income. Trust me, not so many of my age-mates can say the same about their incomes. I figured out some innovative ways to ensure my money lasts the month and, at times, into the next month. In case you are wondering, I do all this and still get to live a happy, content life. I hang out with my friends and family, eat at restaurants, and order the occasional take-outs when I deserve a treat, and for the icing on the cake, I'm debt free!

So, why am I telling you all this?

I have no intention of flaunting my success. I've achieved something many would consider a spectacle, yet in my opinion, this is just everyday life. I want my story to encourage you and remind you that there's never a good or bad place to start in the journey to financial freedom. Start where you are today, and take it one step at a time.

The exciting thing about being in a low place financially is that there's so much room for you to go up. This is what many people never realize. First, you have to accept the reality of where you are financially. Call yourself to that board meeting, and face the facts. This crucial step can be your lightbulb moment. Some people wait until their 40s and 50s when they are hounded by mortgages, bills, school fees, and taxes, to have this moment. You don't have to wait that long. If you do things right, you'll publish your book on how you achieved financial independence in your 20s when you get to that age.

As I mentioned earlier, the academic curriculum didn't help me much in my journey to financial freedom. I tried a bit of trial and error here and there, but eventually, I figured out some simple self-taught methods that got me this far. One important lesson I learned is that most, if not all, of the resources you need to make better financial decisions are already within your reach.

I've spent years studying personal finance, improving my personal spending habits and financial decision-making so much that it has become a hobby. I find it rewarding to teach people about the role of personal finance in the pursuit of financial independence. I pay special attention to young adults because you are at the cusp of greatness. Your life is just getting started, and there's no better way to do it than to start on the right financial footing.

In a way, I consider this my greatest contribution to the advancement of future generations. You might not realize it yet, but you are more prepared and financially literate than many generations ahead of you at this stage in life. You can access resourceful individuals and institutions to help you make better financial decisions today than any other generation before you.

No matter your financial situation, I hope to empower you to a financial awakening that will help you understand the magnitude of responsibility you have regarding your finances, and your life in general.

I believe that you can do better. I believe that you can be better.

Let's do this!

1
FOUNDATIONS OF PERSONAL FINANCE

FOR A BETTER FINANCIAL TODAY

"Money is a tool. Used properly, it makes something
beautiful; used wrong, it makes a mess!"
—Bradley Vinson

*P*eople have varying views about money, mainly influenced by their upbringing or interactions. Unfortunately, for many people, money will always be an enigma, something that's quite difficult to understand. The irony is that even with varying views on money, we all still use money every day.

Learning about money isn't only about everyday activities like how much things cost or how much you should receive as change. It's about understanding how to earn and grow your money. After all, having more money allows you more freedom in terms of obtaining the things you want.

Even as you seek more money, learning how to be responsible is even more important. The interesting thing about money is that while it might be a bit difficult to get your hands on it, losing it is quite easy, hence the need for responsibility. Being responsible with your money also entails budgeting for it, and in case you borrow it, paying it back so it doesn't become a burden.

Let's be honest; being responsible with money isn't something we are all good at. From time to time, you end up with too little money against a long list of things you still need to pay for, yet at the beginning, you had what you might have considered enough money to take care of all your expenses. So, how does this happen? How do you end up in this predicament?

To figure this out, we must go back to a concept we used earlier—understanding money. Did you know that it's actually not your fault that you might not know about things like budgeting, loans, or interest? Our school system was created in such a way that even though we learn so much, money isn't one of those things we are taught. For some reason, they ignore it, especially how to handle your personal money.

Think about it for a moment. You might have learned so much about financial concepts like accounting, auditing, exchange rates, and so on, yet no one ever cared to teach you stuff like budgeting for your money, saving it, and eventually growing it. To be clear, these three things are crucial to your financial independence. When done correctly, they can help you retire early, relax, and enjoy life while your money works for you instead of working for your money until you grow old.

You are constantly told in school that you need to learn XYZ to succeed in life, yet money has never been included in that list of things to help you become a success. Don't worry, this book will help you change that.

Since you use money every day, you'll learn simple yet effective tips you can implement daily. These simple adjustments can significantly impact your life once you integrate them into your daily routine.

UNDERSTANDING PERSONAL FINANCE

"Money, like emotions, is something you must control to keep your life on the right track."
—Natasha Munson

Despite what you might have been told, no one is ever too young or old to learn about money. Financial literacy is an important life skill, so learning about money early in life gives you a better chance of making good financial decisions. It's quite unfortunate that so many young people have no clue what financial wellness is. To bridge this gap, it's important to encourage financial education from a young age. Here are some reasons why:

• **Overall Economic Growth**

While we can point fingers at banks and other financial institutions for the global financial crisis of 2008, the fact is that their actions were the collective effects of individuals making terrible financial decisions, primarily because of financial indiscipline. Financial literacy can help you manage your finances effectively in difficult circumstances like the financial crisis or the COVID pandemic.

• **Financial Misdeeds**

Without knowledge of personal financial management, many young adults are entrapped into hardship by the same mistakes people have made for years. We are talking about overdrawn accounts, credit card debt, overdue bills, and so on, with far-reaching effects like poor credit and bankruptcies.

• Budgeting and Savings

Money comes and goes, but if you learn to budget for what you have and save some of it, you'll end up with more money coming in than going. Budgeting and saving teach you an important life skill—discipline. You'll learn that you don't always have to spend everything you have and, more importantly, how to prioritize your spending and put some aside for a rainy day.

• Student Loans

The constantly rising costs have made college education increasingly inaccessible to many students, who plug the deficit through student loans. Without financial awareness, student loans can be a trap that cripples you financially. You should learn about the impact of loan defaults, interest accruing on the loans, and affordable alternatives to student loans.

• A Helping Hand

Young adults should learn the value of giving back to the community. To give back, you must first learn to save, spend wisely, and share with the less fortunate. This lays the foundation for investing in communities and creating more opportunities for future generations.

It's clear that financial literacy is bigger than an individual. If every one of us makes smart decisions with our money, there's so much we can do to uplift and improve our society.

* * *

THE REAL COST OF POVERTY

Poverty makes it difficult to plan long-term, so most, if not all, of your financial decisions are often short-term. Unfortunately, this makes it nearly impossible for you to make any real financial progress. To prove this, let's discuss some common expense items below:

- **Food and Groceries**

First, most poor people can't afford bulk shopping, even though food and groceries account for most of their household incomes. Even when they can, they might not have sufficient storage facilities. Apart from that, for various economic and social reasons, most large food and grocery outlets whose prices are affordable tend to avoid such areas, so your only options are fast-food restaurants and convenience stores. You end up spending more than wealthy households who can buy more and stock for later. On top of that, eating from fast-food restaurants and convenience stores means mainly eating unhealthy food.

- **Health and Medication**

Low-income households face multiple healthcare challenges, and in most cases, you are always one job loss or misfortune away from plunging into extreme poverty. It gets even worse, considering the health concerns arising from an inability to access affordable healthy organic foods.

- **Financial Support**

Payday loans, cash advance companies, credit card companies, rent-to-own shops, and other similar business models understand the credit access problem for low-income households. They offer an immediate solution to long-term problems, which isn't sustainable in the long run.

These organizations thrive in low-income neighborhoods by preying on people's desperation. They know you can't afford to pay the full price, but you can make a small payment and roll over the balance to the following month when you get paid. It might seem convenient, but this is one of the most expensive arrangements, especially if you factor in the interest rates and other transaction costs.

- **Taxation**

Unfortunately, those who don't make enough end up paying even more in taxes. It's not just the local taxes, sales tax, and the like. You also have social tax, where you can't access quality services by living in a certain neighborhood. Therefore, you can either pay more to access better services in a different neighborhood or contend with insufficient or —at times— no services.

- **Raising a Family**

If you have kids, especially younger preschool kids, you must factor their well-being into your housing costs. Child care and rent can consume up to half your income or even higher. Where child care isn't an option, you'll enlist the help of a family member or a trusted neighbor, which also comes with some costs. Alternatively, one parent might have to quit and stay at home, reducing the overall household income and increasing strain and pressure on the working parent.

- **Housing**

One of the harsh realities of poverty is that you can't own a house. Even if you wanted to, most lenders would frown at your credit score. You'll also struggle to raise the deposit required, which is generally higher for people with bad credit. Your only option is to rent, watching helplessly as your money disappears into someone else's pockets every month.

• Transportation

First, since you might not be able to afford houses closer to your place of work, you'll be living far away from it. This means you must either depend on public transportation or occasionally supplement your commute with ride-sharing services like Uber.

Transportation costs become inconvenient, especially if you need to own a car. You must think of maintenance costs, insurance, fuel, and, if you are getting it on loan, the cost of financing. At the end of the month, you are spending too much on transportation just to enjoy a few inconveniences.

• Communication

Mobile data and prepaid plans are the norms in low-income households. On the other hand, high-income households mostly use postpaid plans bundled into the latest devices, giving them more freedom and options in communication devices. They also have access to home WiFi services, giving them more variety in connectivity. In a world heavily reliant on interconnectivity and prompt communication, you miss lots of opportunities by simply being unreachable.

As you can see above, even though living from one paycheck to the next might seem like you are getting by, the sad reality is that it's also the easiest way to end up deeper in debt. Low incomes and increasingly high living cost further worsen the situation for poor households.

* * *

LOTTERIES AND POVERTY

Winning the lottery isn't always the glamorous story many think it is. In fact, it could be the beginning of your financial troubles. Cases of young adults winning the lottery and blowing it all on partying, cars, drugs, jewelry, and lavish vacations are widespread these days.

There's the incident of a 19-year-old who won an $19.8 million jackpot but ended up working in a slaughterhouse for a few hundred dollars a week.

We also have the couple that divorced soon after a $215.9 million jackpot, splurging on designer wear, expensive houses, and exotic cars. This couple thought they had so much money they enrolled their daughter in an expensive private school. When the money ran out, the wife had to become an employee in a salon she opened. On the other hand, the husband's rockstar dreams were no more than a pipe dream, draining most of their money in the process. Ultimately, between the two, all they had to their names was $10.

The examples above clearly indicate that no amount of money can protect you from financial illiteracy. But if financial literacy is lacking, why don't our schools teach it to students? Clearly, sound knowledge of personal finance could have made a big difference in the lives of these lottery winners, right?

One of the reasons why schools don't teach personal finance is because we are still stuck with the old mindset where kids are encouraged to study, graduate, and hope to get a good salary, great benefits, work for several years, and retire. This mentality no longer applies unless you've been living under a rock these past few years. Our generation no longer believes in giving all your productive adult life to a single company, so you can earn a generous sendoff package and a pension when you retire. If anything, most people spend no more than three years in a job today.

Kids have to fill the personal finance knowledge gap from their parents, most of whom aren't exactly the best at managing personal finances. If you grow up in an entrepreneurial household, for example, you have a better chance of understanding finances better than someone who was raised in a family getting by on minimum wages.

It gets worse; even the teachers lack the financial competency to impart this knowledge. It's challenging to teach students about personal finances when the teachers themselves, at a personal level, are struggling with basic financial literacy concepts. Before asking them to teach kids about personal finances, we must educate the instructors.

None of these situations are helped by the fact that in many households, money is still a taboo subject that only adults can discuss. Even then, these conversations are hardly healthy or constructive. This explains why most people lie to their friends and family members about the true state of their finances.

FUNDAMENTAL PRINCIPLES EVERYONE SHOULD KNOW

You can make significant strides in your life by understanding the following fundamental principles of personal finance:

- **Retirement Planning** — Start planning for retirement today. It might seem too far in the future, but the cumulative value of investing early will yield greater returns when you retire.

- **The Value of Credit** — Pay attention to your credit score. Clear your bills and debt balances on time, and do all you can to maintain a good credit score.
- **Emergency Planning** — Emergencies are a way of life. The best way to work around their unpredictability is to ensure adequate insurance coverage and save money in your emergency fund every month.
- **Prudent Spending** — Strive to spend less than you earn every month and save as much as possible. The point is to ensure that your monthly expenses never exceed your income.
- **Income Maximization** — Saving some money every month is awesome. However, there's a limit to the amount you can save each month from your income. A better approach would be looking for additional sources of revenue. Negotiate for a raise, start a side hustle, look for a better job, and so on. Diversifying your sources of income will give you more room for financial growth.
- **Financial Literacy** — Make a habit of learning about money and investments. Read blogs and books, sign up for webinars, and follow some famous financial authors to further your insight into financial investments.
- **Be Organized** — Track all your financial accounts, from credit cards to loan and investment accounts, to understand how your money moves around. There are lots of budgeting programs that can help with this.
- **Risk Mitigation** — Risk is a normal part of finance. Carefully assess the level and type of investment risk

before you commit your money. More importantly, understand your risk appetite to determine the kind of investments suitable for your risk profile.
- **Understand Your Taxes** — The last thing you want is a run-in with the IRS. Try to learn about taxes, especially the adjustments necessary for every investment you make. Each investment attracts some form of taxation, and paying taxes to Uncle Sam is mandatory.
- **Employment Benefits** — You can quickly reduce your monthly expenses or taxes by maximizing the utility value of your medical insurance, flexible spending accounts, or 401(k) plans.

While there are many financial tips that you might come across in the future, the points above cover the most critical issues that will set you on the path to financial independence from an early age and guarantee your financial security in the future.

* * *

LIVING BELOW YOUR MEANS

Your total expenses should never exceed your income every month. That's what living below your means is about, and it is by far the simplest way to escape the paycheck-to-paycheck life and avoid or overcome debt.

Signs You Are Not Living Below Your Means

Many people today don't live below or even within their means. This problem is mainly fueled by pressure from social media, because of which you try to live up to unrealistic expectations, usually from people who don't even care about or know you. Here are some indicative signs you should watch out for:

1. **No Emergency Fund** — If you don't have any savings for emergencies, you'll struggle financially in an emergency. Another sign of trouble is if you can't save anything from your paycheck.
2. **Credit Card Debt** — This is when you struggle to clear credit card debt, so it keeps piling up monthly.
3. **Unnecessary Splurges** — Constantly treating yourself to a lavish lifestyle on your credit card, digging yourself deeper into debt.

How to Turn Things Around

Acknowledge that you are doing poorly financially, and take bold measures to turn things around. Here are some valuable tips you can start practicing right away:

1. **Budgeting** — A budget gives you better control over your finances. Review it weekly or monthly to identify areas where you can cut down your expenditure. Common items you can review include online shopping, restaurant meals, and entertainment expenditure.
2. **Savings Plan** — Start saving through automated deductions from your paycheck to your savings account. Increase your savings by reducing your monthly expenditure. Review your expenses, such as insurance, internet bills, and phone plans, for affordable options, and start building an emergency fund.
3. **Drive an Inexpensive or Used Car** — Research the market for a decent used car. Be careful in your

search, however, because a used car with many underlying issues can be more expensive than a new car.

4. **Rethink Your Apartment** — Consider a smaller house or an affordable neighborhood. If you are spending more than 30% of your gross income on insurance, taxes, mortgages, and other costs related to the house, it's time to rethink that house.

5. **Avoid Credit Cards** — Credit cards are convenient, but they also conveniently drag you into debt. Pay off the cards with the highest interest first, and consider drastic measures like cutting up the card or locking them away until you pay off the debt.

6. **More Sources of Income** — Supplement your income with a side hustle. Aim for passive sources of income because these will eventually earn you more money with minimal input.

7. **Lifestyle Review** — Rethink your lifestyle. There's nothing wrong with pretending that you don't have money. Pretending to be broke can get you out of unnecessary commitments where you'd have spent money you don't have and end up factually broke.

Delete your card details from online stores to eliminate the ease of confirming purchases. If you feel the urge to indulge in an impulse purchase, put the idea off for a few days. In most cases, you'll move on from that idea.

Appreciate what you already have, so you don't spend more on shoes, clothes, or a second car.

* * *

NEEDS VS. WANTS

A need is anything you must have to survive. The definition of a need can also include living a relatively comfortable life. For example, food is a basic need. You need food to survive. However, eating at an expensive restaurant isn't a basic need. Ideally, needs are the basic requirements for your survival.

Wants are primarily luxuries. They are not essential items; you can still live a normal and healthy life without luxury cars and vacations. As in the example above, some needs can be classified as wants depending on circumstances. For example, a simple house is a basic need. A lavish mansion, however, becomes a want as it satisfies your desire for luxury.

Distinguishing Needs from Wants

The difference between needs and wants isn't usually clear, especially where comfort is involved, as we've seen in the examples above. You should remember that absence of needs can breed negative consequences, but not so much where wants are not provided.

Basic food, shelter, and clothing are all you need to survive. Over the years, utilities like internet connection, mobile phones, electricity, water, and sewage have gained such prominence in our modern lives that we can also consider them as needs.

Wants give you the benefit or convenience of choice. We can explain this with needs that become wants by choice or convenience: bars and takeouts (food), expensive home décor and furniture (shelter), expensive designer clothes, or high-speed internet just for home entertainment, yet you don't work from home.

If you're in doubt about needs and wants, ask yourself: What would happen if you were to go a whole week without this item?

The main reason for establishing these differences is to avoid spending money on things you don't need.

* * *

ASSETS AND LIABILITIES

"You must know the difference between an asset and a liability, and buy assets...rich people acquire assets. Poor and middle-class people acquire liabilities, but they think they are assets."
—*Robert Kyosaki*

An asset is something you own that has or will increase in economic value in the future. Assets can be tangible, intangible, current, or fixed. Tangible assets are those you can see or touch, like the equipment you use in your business, while intangible assets don't have such physical features, for example, your domain name or a website or blog that earns you some income.

A current asset is liquid in that you can convert it to cash in a year or less, for example, the cash you have in the bank or your wallet at home. On the other hand, fixed assets are useful for more than a year, for example, your business premise or cars used in running your business.

Common examples of assets you can relate to include businesses you own, rental or real estate property, and dividends from your stock investments.

Liabilities are debts you owe other people or companies. They must be paid back, or they can exercise any right to get their money back, including repossessing your property.

Liabilities can be short-term (current), meaning that they must be cleared within a year, or long-term, meaning it will take more than a year to clear the debts.

Common liabilities include bad debts (we'll discuss this in the next chapter), mortgages, credit card debt, or taxes if you still owe the government.

Note that cars and houses can be assets or liabilities, depending on whether they bring you income. Your car is a liability if you only use it to commute or let it sit in your garage. It is an asset if you rent it out, use it for deliveries, or ride-sharing businesses like Uber or Lyft.

Your house is a liability if you only pay mortgages or bills on it every month. It is an asset, however, if you get rental income from it, even if you only rent out one room or the garage.

It's important to understand these differences so that you can channel more money from liabilities to grow your asset profile. This is one of the simplest ways to secure your financial future.

* * *

AVOIDING COMMON FINANCIAL MISTAKES

Let's face it; people make mistakes all the time. Financial mistakes you make today could have a significant impact on your future. Well, instead of learning the hard way, let's learn about some of these mistakes now, so you don't fall into the same trap:

Mistake #1: Misusing Credit Cards

Solution: While credit cards give you convenience, never forget that they are loans and must be repaid in full, all the time.

Mistake #2: Hoarding Unnecessary Memberships

Solution: Review your lifestyle, and cancel the memberships that don't add value. For example, there's no need to pay for high-speed internet when you're only at home over the weekends. Downgrade or find a pay-as-you-go plan.

Mistake #3: Impulse Buying

Solution: Particularly for large purchases, it's always wise to compare prices first, then buy the item later. This simple approach can save you hundreds of dollars every year.

Mistake #4: That New Car

Solution: Did you know that cars lose at least 20% of their value within the first year? If anything, the dealership cannot buy the vehicle from you at the price they sold it to you, even if you drove it out for a minute after buying it and decided to return it. Ideally, good used vehicles offer more value for money than new cars.

Mistake #5: Ignoring Financial Education

Solution: Our schools barely touch on the important aspects of personal finance. There are many alternatives to help you learn about personal finances. From webinars to blogs and YouTube videos, you can educate yourself in your free time.

Mistake #6: Life Without a Plan or a Budget

Solution: The simplest approach you can implement right away is the 50:30:20 guide. In this case, you allocate 50% of your income to needs, 30% to wants, and 20% to savings, investments, and debt repayment.

Mistake #7: Buying a House You Weren't Ready For

Solution: A new house is a commitment for maybe 20-30 years, yet you haven't factored in maintenance and utility costs. To know if you can afford the home, ensure your total monthly expenditure on it, including mortgages, expenses, and utility bills, does not exceed 36% of your income before taxes.

Mistake #8: Paycheck-to-Paycheck Living

Solution: If you are living paycheck-to-paycheck, you are one illness, accident, job loss, or any other misfortune away from poverty. Review your expenses to find ways through which you can save some money, and start putting some aside for a rainy day.

Mistake #9: Money is a Taboo Subject

Solution: Discuss your finances regularly if you are planning your life with someone. This includes your goals and priorities, so you devise a good strategy to achieve them. Otherwise, you'll become another statistic in the growing list of relationships that broke down because of financial misunderstanding.

Mistake #10: Paying the Minimum Debt Balance

Solution: The minimum balance won't get you out of debt soon. Instead, review your budget and find areas you can scale down, and use the money to reduce your debt balance every month.

* * *

EDUCATION AFTER HIGH SCHOOL

The earlier you start preparing for life after high school, the easier it might be for you to figure out your options and plan for them accordingly. Let's discuss your main options below:

Trade School

This is a viable and affordable option if you don't wish to pursue a four-year college course to kickstart your journey to a well-paid career. Many students prefer trade school because it allows you to focus on specific subjects that align with your career path instead of wasting time on general courses whose content you can quickly learn online.

Pros:

- You can focus on career-relevant training and courses
- Professional development through hands-on training
- Specialized training gives you industry-relevant knowledge and skills
- Spend a shorter time completing your course
- Better learning experience since classes aren't crowded

Cons:

- Fewer financing opportunities compared to colleges and universities
- Lack of variety compared to lots of 4-year college programs limits your options
- Industry-specific learning limits your career options

- The demanding academic schedule leaves little room for anything else
- The oversaturated market for entry-level jobs

Despite the challenges above, trade school isn't just a shorter way to your dream career. And it's also one of the most affordable. For example, the average national cost for trade school programs in 2021 was $32,000. By comparison, you can spend more than three times this figure on a four-year college.

Community College

These colleges offer two-year academic programs that you can use as a stepping stone to higher education. Let's weigh some of the pros and cons below:

Pros:

- Affordability, with most junior colleges costing under $2,000 a semester
- Easier to major in the desired field of study
- Flexibility, especially for students who work and study
- Lower student turnover compared to universities
- Experienced and widely accomplished instructors
- Smaller classes allow students better access to instructors

Cons:

- Don't have the liveliest of social scenes compared to universities
- two-year college curriculum isn't as elaborate as a four-year university curriculum

- Lack of interest from students can result in boring learning sessions

In 2021, the average cost of tuition for a community college was $1,865 a semester, or a total of $7,460. Notably, even in Indiana, where community college is considerably more expensive than the national average, it was still within a reasonable range, with in-state tuition costing around $4,380 and out-of-state tuition $8,460. Even better, tuition-free education programs are available in California, Delaware, Indiana, Kentucky, Maryland, Minnesota, Missouri, New York, Oklahoma, Oregon, Rhode Island, Tennessee, and Washington.

Public State College

These are state-funded universities and colleges. The choice of public vs. private college comes down to your circumstances and academic preferences. We'll review each option's pros and cons to help you determine the most suitable option.

Pros:

- Exciting college lifestyle due to the large student body
- More employment opportunities on campus
- Diversity in academic choices
- Lower tuition fees compared to private colleges

Cons:

- Overcrowding
- The large student population makes it challenging to receive one-on-one attention

- Difficulty in getting administrative support because of the large population
- Enrollment challenges in some classes, which fill up on a first-come-first-served basis

For the 2021-2022 academic year, it will cost you, on average, $10,740 for in-state residency, or $27,560 for out-of-state residency, to enroll in most public-state colleges. Room and boarding costs vary from college to college, though they generally depend on personal choices like your meal plans or whether you choose to live on campus. Either way, you'll spend around $11,950 in a public state college compared to $13,620 for private colleges.

Private College

While public colleges get most of their funds from the state, private colleges are funded independently or through private investors and donors. For this reason, it's generally more expensive to attend a private college than a state-sponsored public college. Here are some pros and cons of attending a private college:

Pros:

- They are primarily close-knit communities, especially for the alumni
- Rigorous activities geared towards academic excellence
- Smaller classes to facilitate better instructor-student interaction
- Sizeable financial aid packages, especially for outstanding students

Cons:

- The student population may not be as diverse as public state colleges
- They are too pricey for most families, especially without financial aid packages
- Limited options when choosing majors and other special programs

For the 2021-2022 academic year, it might cost you, on average, $38,070 to enroll in a private college, with some prestigious private colleges charging even higher. Note that these costs can also vary according to the major you intend to pursue.

YOU'RE GOING TO SCHOOL—WHAT NEXT?

With the options above, your next move is to choose the right institution, not just because you love it but because you can also afford it. College or an alternative is a simple decision. Funding it, however, is a different game altogether. Here are some helpful tips to plan your way through college without straining your pockets in the process:

• Community College

This is the shortest and most affordable way to get your degree. Enroll for general courses at a community college, then transfer to your desired school for specific classes. Find out, however, whether the credits are transferable because not all institutions allow that. This could also help you graduate earlier by avoiding courses that don't add value to your degree.

• Dual Enrollment

You can save on costs, where possible, by enrolling in some college classes while still in high school. This earns you some credits earlier than most students who wait to take those classes in college.

• Affordable Housing

It's always cheaper to live in off-campus housing. However, if your home is closer to the institution, you can commute to school. Living in dorms might offer some convenience but also increase costs like transport, food, utilities, security, and many other miscellaneous expenses.

• Books and Equipment

You don't have to buy new stuff. Borrow those you can, or check out some of the used textbook and equipment stores. Besides you can also download some books online for free.

• Start Earning

See if you qualify for the work-study programs available in school. Other options include part-time jobs, remote freelancing jobs, or becoming a resident advisor, where your college compensates you in some way. Cooperative learning programs are also quite popular, helping you work or study full-time while still getting paid.

• Additional Cost-Cutting Measures

As education becomes more expensive over time, other smart approaches to limit your expenditure include applying for athletic, academic, need-based, or any other scholarships and signing up for government aid through FAFSA. Use campus or public transport to avoid unnecessary car costs like maintenance, parking, gas, and insurance. More importantly, stay away from credit cards if you don't know how to use them effectively.

Most students will apply for student loans. Remember that this is a debt, so be responsible with it. The earlier you start paying it back, the better. If you complete your course but still have some money left, refund it to your lender, giving you a lower balance to pay back.

When College Becomes a Scam

It's increasingly challenging for many students to afford college. Rising college tuition has pushed many people to alternatives, leaving us to wonder whether college is worth the financial input today. Here are some possible reasons why you might need to rethink going to college:

• Rising Costs

It's not just the fees that have gone up tremendously. The costs of student loans, boarding and accommodation, books, and other supplies are impractical for most students, especially since you end up in more debt by the time you graduate.

• Impracticality of Degrees

We live in an age where some of the biggest global brands like Google, Apple, and Tesla don't care much about degrees and instead favor practical and other skills learned through mentorships, training, or self-taught.

• The Remote Class

Why pay so much to attend college when you could learn so much online? Even though COVID supercharged the rapid growth of remote classes, easy access to the internet has helped many people learn valuable skills through YouTube and other online educational sites without necessarily attending college.

• Follow the Money

Today's unfortunate truth is that business needs and financial greed have overrun the once noble cause of imparting knowledge to young minds. Colleges today focus mostly on growing their business enterprises at the expense of students, most of whom end up in debt.

Ultimately, this doesn't mean that you ignore college altogether. Whether Amazon and Google want it, your degree will still be useful in many other top companies. However, with the information above, you should broaden your horizon and consider alternatives that don't force you into debt, especially if you can't afford to pay your way through college.

2
DEBT

THE WORST TYPE OF POVERTY

*L*et me tell you a story of Sam, this guy I dated back in high school and college.

You see, Sam was born into a family that was neither well off nor poor. Given my parents' background, I respected Sam's dad. He put four kids through school and took care of the household on a full-time job and side hustle, as Sam's mom was a housewife.

I knew they had credit card debt in the tens of thousands but still got the kids into travel sports. Travel sports are expensive, especially with trip costs like food and accommodation. It would be practical if the kids trained to become professional athletes, but none were.

Sam was also on three other sports teams, so naturally, he ate a lot. One day he called, complaining about this fight with his mom. He threw a fit because she portioned dinner and demanded that he pay for the extra pizza slice he ate since everyone had been allocated two slices. I won't go into the specifics, but Sam was livid!

Money was a taboo subject in that home. No one talked about it, ever, probably because anything financial was left to the dad. Funny enough, his wife had a math degree from a prestigious college that is notoriously difficult to get into. This is someone with expert knowledge on money matters, yet all this potential was wasted.

I figured all this out because Sam was perennially broke, so some of these conversations would unwittingly come up. When I say perennially, I mean the many times I'd cook and deliver dinner to his place since he didn't have anything to eat; I'd send him some money to top up his lease deposit; or, and I say this with a straight face, to pay for dinner. With Sam and his money, there was always something. Unfortunately, Sam devoted most of his time to lacrosse and wasn't doing well academically, which would eventually be why he was placed on academic suspension.

It hurt that I worked hard for the little I spared to bail him out from time to time. I used to work in the school dining hall—nothing glamorous about it, but it got some extra cash into my pocket. I wasn't working out of struggle or anything; I figured this was a smart way to get more money than I already had, to invest or buy better food.

Concerned about his endless struggles, I once shared with Sam how picking up some hours in the dining hall could help cover his grocery needs for a few days. His response shocked me! He scoffed at my idea! He laughed it off in my face so hard; I've never felt that offended. Here was someone who, without my help, could have possibly starved but was too embarrassed to work a few hours in the school dining hall. In fact, he said he would NEVER work in a dining hall.

People work minimum wage jobs all the time, yet standing before me was an idiot so high in his pride that he'd rather starve. That's when I realized that life with Sam meant doing all the heavy lifting while he pursued his passions and hobbies, regardless of whether he was any good at them or bringing in any income from them. A life of debt and stress wasn't what I envisioned for myself, so for this and other reasons, I left.

* * *

UNDERSTANDING DEBT

Debt arises when you borrow some money and persists until the day you pay it in full. When you borrow $50 from a friend, you'll only pay them back $50, and your debt is settled. However, this doesn't apply to formal debt like mortgages. In such instances, you must repay the amount plus interest.

Interest is the lender's compensation against the risk that you might default on the loan. The longer you stay without clearing the loan, the more interest you'll pay. Thus, interest encourages you to pay back the loan faster.

THE GRIM PICTURE

Most people are in debt, and given the economic uncertainties, the situation could worsen. How bad is it? The total national consumer debt was $14.14 trillion in 2019 but had burgeoned to $15.31 trillion in 2021. Most people have been struggling with mortgages, student loans, and credit card debt, especially coming off the effect of the Covid pandemic. But how did we end up in this position? Why do people end up in debt?

The debt position above doesn't paint an encouraging picture, especially for young adults. What can you do to ensure you don't end up deep in debt? Let's look at some common reasons why people get in debt below:

• Low Income

If your bills exceed your income, you are on a slippery slope to debt. Unless you do something about it and increase your income, you'll end up in debt.

• Inadequate Savings

It doesn't matter how much you earn; always try to save for emergencies. A good savings plan means having 3-6 months' worth of household expenses in a savings account.

• Income-Expense Mismatch

If you are earning less than you used to, reduce your expenses. This can also happen due to poor money management skills and bills outrunning your income.

• Unplanned Expenditure

This is an interesting one that many people are guilty of— spending before you earn. Perhaps someone promised you some money tomorrow, so you spend what you have today, hoping they'll come through for you. Unfortunately, things change very fast in life, and you might not receive a cent of what you were promised. As a rule of thumb, never make plans with money not already in your pocket.

• Financial Illiteracy

Many people don't understand the dynamics of money, how to earn it, grow it, or spend it wisely. They make costly financial mistakes that take years to resolve.

• Medical Emergencies

If you don't have medical insurance, any medical procedure that involves hospitalization will almost certainly plunge you into debt. Some specialists accept credit card payments or some form of financing arrangement, but this is a basically loan.

• Inflation

The rising cost of living means it's more expensive to buy the same things you used to, on the same income level. For example, suppose something that used to cost $20 is now $25, but your income hasn't changed. In that case, you will struggle to afford the same lifestyle, especially since the immediate impact is usually felt on everyday expenditures like gas and food.

TYPES OF DEBT

Debt is either good or bad. Naturally, people have a negative perception of debt, so it's difficult to see how any debt could be good. However, we'll explain the difference between the two to help you better understand debt.

Good Debt

Good debt includes mortgages, loans to grow your business or education loans. A mortgage goes towards eventually owning a home, which you could even rent out. Business loans give you the financial muscle to compete favorably and meet customer needs. Education loans empower you by putting you through school and gaining useful skills, despite your financial challenges.

Bad Debt

Bad debt is borrowing to buy something that, unlike good debts, doesn't earn you money. This includes depreciating assets like a personal car. Note that purchasing a vehicle for business use doesn't fall in this category if you earn from using the car. Bad debts include purchases like furniture, expensive food, and designer clothes, mainly financed through credit cards.

Ultimately, whether a debt is good or bad depends on individual circumstances. Note that good debts can easily turn into bad debts if you default on the payment.

AVOIDING BAD DEBTS

Even if you don't have all the money you need, it's still possible to avoid debt. Having explained the difference between good and bad debts above, let's discuss some simple tips to help you avoid crippling debt:

- Always have a savings or emergency plan
- Review your personal budget and focus on needs instead of wants
- Create and follow a reasonable monthly budget
- Avoid credit card debt by paying for stuff in cash
- Stop using your credit card for cash advances
- Pay credit card balances in full
- Reduce the number of credit cards you own
- Save money by collecting and redeeming coupons and discount offers where possible
- Do not expand your budget if your income increases
- Track your expenses. This makes it easier to monitor your average expenditure

As you can see above, it's possible to avoid debt. The underlying factor in each point above is discipline. You can cut down your debt through prudent spending.

HOW TO MANAGE DEBT

If you are deep in debt, you must honor the debt payments and still attend to your bills and other expenses. With the right approach, you can get your finances back on track. Here are some simple debt management measures you can implement right away:

• **Accept Your Reality**

Nothing makes it harder to get out of debt than living in denial. Accept that you are in debt, and create a list of everything you owe, including due dates and interest rates. You can find most of this information in your credit report. The idea here is to perform an honest assessment of your finances.

Compare your debts to your income to figure out how much of your money is consumed by debts. This is called the debt to income ratio (DTI) and is obtained by dividing your total debts by your income and then multiplying by 100.

For example, if your total debt is $1,800 against a monthly income of $3,000, your DTI will be: = (1800 ÷ 3000) x 100 = 60%

This means that 60% of your income is servicing your debt. Since this is quite a chunk of your income, you should consider how to improve things. To clear debts faster, perhaps a second job or a side hustle can come in handy.

Since the DTI helps you track your progress in terms of debt repayment, the end goal is to have a declining DTI.

• Debt Prioritization

Always prioritize high-interest debts like credit card debt because these are more expensive. You could also clear smaller debts first and gradually work on the expensive ones. During this time, avoid using credit cards and limit yourself to cash payments.

• Bill Tracker

Track your bill due dates, especially if you receive multiple paychecks. Combine this with your monthly budget to monitor both bills and household expenditures.

• Bills and Recurrent Expenditure

Fees and penalties for late payments add up to your total debt, making it even harder to clear the outstanding debt. Missing multiple payments can also result in higher interest charged on the amount outstanding. Track your payments on a spreadsheet or mobile app so you never fall behind. Clear missed payments as soon as possible.

• Minimum Expected Payments

Pay more than the minimum to clear debts faster. If this isn't possible, pay the minimum required, so you avoid penalties.

• Emergency Planning

Set up a savings account for emergencies. Start small, with a target of maybe $1,000, then work your way up until you save three to six months' worth of your total household expenses.

• Ask For Help

If things are not getting any better, you have options like debt settlement (settling your debt for less than the amount you owe) or consolidation. Each of these alternatives will have implications on your finances in the future, so discuss those with your credit consultant before making a decision.

Ultimately, if you are at a point where the debt is unbearable, you might have to consider filing for bankruptcy.

* * *

BANKRUPTCY

You might have to declare bankruptcy if you can no longer manage your debts. At this point, there's a good chance you've received a foreclosure notice on your home. Bankruptcy might be the way out, but remember that it will stay on your credit report for 7-10 years. If you are struggling to get reasonable loan rates right now, it will be even more challenging with a bankruptcy on your record.

While there are different types of bankruptcy options for companies, Chapter 7 and Chapter 13 are the common options available to individuals.

In Chapter 7, the courts allow liquidating some of your assets to clear your debts. This means you can retain some assets like clothes, personal items, pensions, or stuff you use in your place of work.

Most of your debts are cleared in this process, and you will no longer be required to repay them. Note, however, that some debts like taxes, child support, and student loans cannot be discharged through this approach. Chapter 7 is generally recommended if you are a low-income earner with limited assets to your name.

In Chapter 13, the courts will allow you to keep your assets, but only on the condition that you repay the debts owed within a set period, usually three to five years. A trustee is assigned to collect your payments and distribute them to your creditors. Chapter 13 is ideal if you wish to buy more time to repay your debts so you don't suffer property seizures or foreclosure while still keeping non-exempt assets.

Whatever your situation, consider other options and only file for bankruptcy as a last resort. Talk to your creditors, and try to negotiate favorable arrangements with them. More often than not, this is usually more affordable than bankruptcy and doesn't leave as much damage on your credit. You'd be surprised that many creditors can prolong your payment term for lower payments; you just have to ask politely.

If you have a mortgage, some lenders suggest a new payment plan, offering to modify your loan by allowing you lower interest for the loan balance—or a forbearance—where they will enable you to postpone loan payments for some time.

Most people don't know this, but even the IRS is always happy to negotiate affordable arrangements on your tax debt, such as a lower tax or a payment plan. The lesson here is that people are always willing to listen, especially if you have kept up your payments from the start but are unable to continue as you had done previously due to unavoidable circumstances.

You must also visit a credit counseling organization to review your situation. The counselor will also suggest feasible alternatives and present a new budget you can use going forward.

If, after this point, bankruptcy is still your preferred move, the attorney will discuss your bankruptcy options and advice on the appropriate one you should file for.

* * *

3

BUDGETING

WHERE'S YOUR MONEY GOING?

"A budget is telling your money where to go,
instead of wondering where it went."
—Dave Ramsey

$\mathcal{M}$y experience in college opened my eyes to the unfortunate reality that most of my generation know nothing about money or priorities. I say, unfortunately, because these were students who would probably go on to become parents. It made me shudder at what lies ahead for future generations.

On many occasions, some of my friends would complain about how they were so low on cash that they had no idea how to make groceries for the week or, even worse, their rent money. I understand that college life is expensive, especially for students without any income source. However, it was absurd that the same people complaining always threw caution to the wind when they had money. You'd not be mistaken to think some of them had won the lottery or came from wealthy families with an unending supply of money.

Out of curiosity, I once tried to find out how my friends spent their money. The conversation didn't take long to figure out why they were constantly broke. I'm not calling anyone out, but when you prioritize wants over needs, there's only one possible outcome. Your money will run out before the month is over.

Most of my friends hardly ever had a budget, so spending below their means was a myth. They partied twice, maybe thrice a week, which meant spending around at least $30 on a night out for the average student. Of course, you'll still have to eat something to quench the munchies after a long night out. Let's say $10 at a fast food restaurant.

If you're spending $40 in one night, that's $80 or $120 a week by someone with no income. We haven't even included miscellaneous expenditures like Uber, tips, or the random monies you lend a friend while drunk that hardly ever get paid back, and you're already looking at $320-$480 a month on partying. This is outrageous, even for most people who have a steady income.

Perhaps my assessment might be biased because I had a different perspective of money by then. Still, I believe it's more sensible and affordable to save money, buy drinks, and have a good time at home with friends than hitting the clubs, whose prices are usually inflated anyway.

To make serious progress in your journey to financial independence, budgeting is one of the essential skills you must learn. This chapter involves more than just learning about budgets. It's also about figuring out the right budget for your lifestyle and how to implement it right away.

FUNDAMENTALS OF BUDGETING

A budget is a detailed guide that helps you plan for your needs within the limits of your income. Budgeting methods are as varied as individual needs. For example, some people budget for everything to the tiniest detail, while others work with categories and apportion their money accordingly. There is no right or wrong way to budget, as long as you hit the ultimate goal of ensuring that all your money is accounted for.

People have varied reasons why they'd need to create a budget. Ultimately, the main purpose of budgeting is to instill financial discipline and, in the process, learn how to be in charge of your money. Contrary to what most people believe, budgeting isn't necessarily about deprivation. It's about your money meeting your needs, whatever those might be.

Human needs, tastes, and preferences change all the time, as do your finances and circumstances in life. Therefore, a reasonable budget should be flexible enough to accommodate these changes. This is one of the reasons why we mentioned earlier that there's no right or wrong way to budget. Budgeting is about your life, so try to personalize it to work for you.

Budgets play an important role in the journey to financial freedom. Therefore, they are valuable tools everyone can benefit from, not only those with messy finances. A budget is your reminder that you can and should live within your means and, in the process, empower your money to work for you.

Following a budget can help you in the following ways:

- Stress relief by making sound financial decisions improves your preparedness for unforeseen challenges.
- Prudent spending habits could help you get out of debt or stay out of debt.
- A budget is incomplete without a savings plan. You are better prepared for vacations, retirement, or huge purchases.

Perhaps one of the greatest benefits of budgeting besides financial discipline is that it can help you understand your behaviors around money and, in the process, your relationship with money. Your relationship with money includes things like how you spend or save, your priorities when you receive some cash, what you do when you don't have money, how you adjust your expenditure according to varying income levels, and so on.

TYPES OF PERSONAL BUDGETS

This section will review common types of budgets you can consider to manage your finances.

• The 50:30:20 Budget

This budget encourages you to distribute all your income accordingly. 50% goes towards needs, 30% to wants, and 20% for savings and paying off debt.

Best for: someone just getting started, as 20% is an ideal place to start.

• The No Budget Budget

This budget generally means not keeping a formal budget but still being able to meet your financial needs.

Best for: carefree people but still maintain financial discipline while at it.

• The Saving First Budget

This budget encourages you to focus on your personal goals by paying yourself first before spending money on other things.

Best for: someone who doesn't mind sacrificing their spending on other things to shore up their savings account.

• The Spending First Budget

The concept of this budget is to save whatever remains after you plan for all your expenses.

Best for: those confident that your monthly expenses are always below your income.

• The Spending Ceiling Budget

The point of this budget is to set a limit for your expenditure and try to stay within it. Once you hit the limit, you can no longer buy anything until the next month.

Best for: someone who doesn't mind reviewing their budget monthly and adjusting accordingly.

• The Zero-Based Budget

In this budget, you ensure that every single cent of your income is budgeted for. You allocate money to each category until you have nothing left.

Best for: individuals who want to be strict with their expenditure.

• The Anti-Budget Budget

The idea behind this budget is to allocate a percentage of your income to savings, then spend whatever remains.

Best for: someone who doesn't need to track their spending, especially if you are disciplined or are not a heavy spender. It could be useful if you live alone and don't yet have many financial commitments.

Note that you can equally combine the benefits of two budgets, for example, the spending ceiling and spending first budget. You might come across these budgets with different names elsewhere, but the end goal is to meet your financial needs.

BUILDING A BUDGET

The secret to successful budgeting is finding a way to track your money. In this section, we'll use the 50:30:20 budget to explain simple steps on how to go about it.

Step #1: Your Income

How much are you bringing home? You are working with the net income, not your gross income, because that has not been adjusted for tax and other deductions.

Step #2: Organization

Now that you are aware of how much you are working with, you need to categorize your expenditure so it's easier to track your money. This will also help you figure out where you can save more money. List everything you spend on, then from the list, create relevant categories.

Step #3: Agenda Setting

Before you review the list above, set realistic financial goals you'd like to achieve in the short-term and long-term. Note that realistic goals don't necessarily have to be cast in stone. Allow yourself some room for flexibility.

Step #4: Planning

Now that your goals are clear, split 50% of your income to needs and mandatory expenditure, 30% to your wants, and 20% to savings and debt repayments.

Step #5: Review and Adjustment

With everything adequately documented, you can move things around where necessary, especially from your wants, and save that money.

Step #6: Regular Review

The budget will only work if you adjust it regularly to ensure you are still on track to achieve your financial goals. For example, if you get a raise or have an emergency expenditure, you must adjust accordingly.

BUDGETING FOR WANTS AND NEEDS

You won't always have enough money for your needs and wants. From time to time, you'll have to make some sacrifices to meet both or one over the other. Here are some simple tips to help you budget for each of these categories:

• Quit Impulsive Spending

Just because you like something and it's available doesn't mean you have to buy it immediately. To stop impulse buying, practice leaving your credit card at home, especially when shopping or going for a random stroll. You could also shop when time is limited, like during your lunch break, so you can only focus on important things.

- **Suitable Budget**

Make sure your monthly budget allocates a reasonable amount of money for both wants and needs, so you don't feel like you are neglecting one. Remember that wants arc just as important as your needs.

- **Specificity**

Be specific in your budget to avoid ambiguity. For example, instead of bundling all your meals under the food category, go a step further and create subcategories like eating out, groceries, or ordering in.

- **Responsible Credit Card Usage**

It's easier to go overboard when swiping your card than using cash. There's nothing wrong with a random splurge here and there on your credit card. However, try to limit yourself so you don't spend more than you can afford. As a rule of thumb, pay back your credit card expenses as soon as possible.

COMMON BUDGETING MISTAKES AND HOW TO AVOID THEM

When we talk of budgeting, it doesn't necessarily mean being a penny-pincher or denying yourself the small pleasures in life. A proper budget allows you to meet all your needs while enjoying an exciting life. It's all about discipline and knowing when to stop. Unfortunately, we make some budgeting mistakes all the time that make it harder to achieve our financial goals. Here are eight of the most common mistakes you should be on the lookout for:

Mistake #1: Paying for subscriptions you hardly use

There's only one solution here—cancel them!

Mistake #2: Ignoring your taxes

Always budget with your after-tax income because that's the money you actually have.

Mistake #3: Not budgeting for entertainment

Even though you are trying to save money, life without fun is dull. Try and allocate some money for some enjoyment.

Mistake #4: Focusing too much on savings

Granted, you want to save some money, but there's only so much you can save on your current income. Instead of squeezing every penny out of your budget, tap into the gig economy and start a side hustle.

Mistake #5: No plan for emergencies

Always create room in your budget for an emergency savings account. You'd rather have that money and not need it than need it and not have it.

Mistake #6: Complicating the budget

The budget should be simple enough for you to figure out in one glance. Don't complicate it with unrealistic categories.

Mistake #7: Ambiguity

You cannot budget for "around $5,000." You either have $5,000, or you don't. Be specific with the amounts in your budget.

Mistake #8: Ignoring the budget review

True, your budget might work for the first few months, but things change all the time. Prices change your income changes, and so on. Review your budget regularly to factor in these changes.

Perhaps the biggest budgeting mistake of them all is not having one in the first place. Without a budget, your approach to finances and life, in general, is guesswork. This is the easiest way of planning to fail.

THE EMERGENCY BUDGET

An emergency budget is like having your own insurance coverage that you can use when things are not going as intended. An ideal budget should be worth three to six months of your total monthly expenses, though it can also vary according to your income, lifestyle, and needs.

Some instances where an emergency budget could come in handy include the following:

- Unexpected but necessary travel
- Medical expenses
- Emergency repairs at home
- Car repairs after an accident
- Living expenses if you lose your job

If you are ever in a situation where you have to use the emergency fund, you'll also have to adjust your spending to replenish the emergency budget.

Now that you know what the emergency budget is, how do you create one? Below are some simple steps to guide you:

Step 1: Needs Assessment

This budget will only be realistic if it aligns with your needs. Once you've determined how much you need, the next step is to sell stuff you don't need to kickstart the fund.

Step 2: Budget Review

Carefully track your money every month to identify areas where you can make savings and divert that money to the emergency fund. This is where things like canceling some subscriptions will be useful.

Step 3: Setting Goals

Going by the money you already have in your account from the steps above, how much more do you need to reach your target? Do the math, then come up with a plan to achieve it. This is where you decide the right amount to set aside every week or month to achieve your goal.

Step 4: Managing Accounts

Open a savings account separate from your regular accounts. The point here is to keep your emergency fund out of sight. You can also create automatic payments from your checking account to your emergency account.

Step 5: Honor Your Budget

Now that everything is in place, it's time to do the work. Follow your budget accordingly, and make adjustments where necessary. If you get a raise, increase the amount that goes to your emergency fund.

DOWNSIZE AND SUBSTITUTE

One of the secrets to financial success in life is to know when it's right to downsize or opt for substitutes. More often than not, we make the mistake of spending more because we got a raise. This is called lifestyle inflation. It's another easy way to mess up your finances and your life.

If you ever end up in a situation where finances are tight, you can review your lifestyle and downsize a few things that will eventually help you save money. Let's highlight some areas where you can make significant savings below:

- **Your House**

One thing you'll realize as you grow older is that there's always an affordable house that can offer the same benefits you enjoy where you currently live, so move out of the house where you now live. As a rule of thumb, try to spend less than 30% of your income on housing.

- **Your Household**

Most people can't admit it, but we hoard many things that we barely or never use. From old electronics to furniture and appliances, sell these items instead of keeping them in the house for no reason.

- **Your Expenses**

This is another area where you'll save more on your monthly budget, especially after downsizing your house. Individually, it might not seem like much money, but you'll be pleasantly surprised when you add the savings from all expense items.

- **Your Car**

Ditch the car altogether and use public transport. If you can't do that, downsize your car for one with considerably lower maintenance costs. Your auto expenses should not exceed 10% of your income.

* * *

4

INSURANCE

EXPECT THE UNEXPECTED

*I*nsurance is a subject you always see in the news, in regular conversations, and so on. It's such an important part of life that it's a shame many people never stop to wonder what it's all about and why they should have it. From your house to your car and even your life, there's an insurance policy for anything you can think of. So, how come you've never given it some thought?

An insurance contract is an agreement outlined in a policy document whereby you, the insured, should receive some compensation from the insurer in the event of a misfortune for which you are insured.

As a binding contract, there's a thin line between what your insurer can pay for and what they can't. There are instances where customers have claimed that their insurer abandoned them. Yet, in the real sense, the nature of the risk for which the customer sought reimbursement or compensation wasn't within their insurance contract.

Insurers understand that there are different levels of risk involved in any undertaking. This is why they pool client risks together, making it easier to address your claims and offer affordable premiums.

HOW INSURANCE WORKS

Insurance covers you against the possibility of incurring specific risks in your contract. Naturally, misfortune won't befall everyone at the same time. For this reason, the insurer spreads risks by collecting premiums from different clients, effectively reducing the cost of insuring each client.

In some cases, insurance is mandatory, such as mortgages and loans, to protect lenders against borrower default. Motor vehicle insurance protects both the car owner or driver and other parties who might be involved in an accident.

IMPORTANCE OF INSURANCE

Insurance guarantees a good reprieve in case of any misfortune to the insured. Let's go deeper and highlight some reasons why, at a personal level, you should buy insurance:

- **Peace of Mind** — You are at peace knowing that your family, property, or investments are protected in case of a crisis. With medical insurance, for example, you don't have to worry about digging into your pocket to seek treatment.
- **Financial Security** — Insurance is your first line of defense in the event of an emergency. Accidents, injuries, illness, or death can have far-reaching

financial effects on your family. Apart from the emotional trauma, you might also have a hefty financial burden. Retirement policies encourage long-term savings from your income, which you receive in retirement as your pension.

- **Create a Savings Culture** — There are many insurance policies to save for expenses like college tuition. These usually have money-back policies where you get some of the money back after a few years.
- **Investing in Your Future** — Ultimately, insurance protects you against uncertainties. The future could be two minutes from now or twenty years. As the sole breadwinner, your untimely demise could usher your family into poverty. Insurance protects not just your future but also that of your dependents.

INSURANCE TYPES AND SIGNIFICANCE

There are different types of insurance policies for various customer needs. Your search for an insurer should be about getting the best value for your money. Let's look at some of the insurance categories below:

- **Health Insurance**

Healthcare is one of the crucial aspects of life whose costs have steadily increased over the years. Depending on the procedure, a hospital visit could cost anywhere between a few hundred to thousands or even millions of dollars.

Insurers usually have agreements with some healthcare providers, so if your favorite hospital or physician is not on the approved list of providers, they might not pay for your medical costs.

Find out any additional costs you might incur apart from the insurance premiums. Most additional fees are charged at the point of contact with your care provider, for example, copay or coinsurance and deductibles.

• Auto Insurance

Auto insurance covers you against financial risks involving your car. Driving a car without basic auto insurance is illegal. Auto insurance coverage varies according to deductibles, amount of coverage taken, and unique benefits.

Your insurance coverage should protect you against the following risks:

1. Damage to someone's property
2. Bodily injuries from the accident
3. Damage to your vehicle
4. Cost of treating injuries sustained in the accident
5. Damages in an accident caused by someone whose insurance coverage isn't sufficient to cover the cost or doesn't have insurance at all

Auto insurance policies typically include any family members named as drivers in your contract or anyone else driving the car with your consent, other than the policyholder.

• Homeowners/ Rental Insurance

Homeowners insurance protects your house against theft and other kinds of damage. It's such an important policy that it's impossible to get a mortgage without it. Insurers consider your potential to file a claim by assessing the condition of the house, the neighborhood, and the possible history of claims by previous residents on that property.

This policy is customizable to your household needs. A basic policy should cover interior and exterior damage to the property, liability for injuries or damages, and accommodation to a different facility if your house is to be repaired or rebuilt.

- **Life Insurance**

Life insurance offers financial protection to your loved ones if you die while the policy is still active. Apart from the lump sum in the eventuality of your demise, it can also be helpful for a funeral, medical, college, and other expenses. You can also list a charitable organization as a beneficiary.

Most people don't have emergency savings accounts, so this can be a good alternative. Besides, your policy doesn't necessarily have to be for the benefit of your beneficiaries. You can also cash out the policy by withdrawing the benefits or taking a loan against the policy.

Life insurance is a worthy investment if you fit into the following categories:

- You are a caregiver
- You have a mortgage
- You are a stay-at-home parent
- You are servicing a mortgage
- You have a co-signed student loan
- You are an income-earning parent

When discussing your options with an insurer, aim for a cover that guarantees you 10-30 times the value of your income at maturity. As an investment in your future, the earlier you start, the better the long-term prospects in the policy.

• Travel Insurance

Travel insurance is not mandatory but could save you from financial trauma. This policy helps frequent travelers with flight cancellations, missing or misplaced luggage, and medical emergencies abroad.

Discuss your options at length with your insurer, especially on exclusions. For example, some insurers don't cover pre-existing medical conditions, while others cover them only if you meet some preconditions.

• Pet Insurance

Medical care for pets can be expensive, especially when they need special attention. Pet insurance takes care of such costs. Pet insurance primarily covers unexpected illnesses, accidental injuries, dental illnesses, chronic conditions, surgery, prescription medicine, cancer treatment, diagnostics, and fees incurred during emergencies. Talk to your insurer about the cost of additional benefits like pregnancy or breeding costs, behavioral modification therapy, or alternative treatments. Find out what the policy doesn't cover because this is where many pet owners make assumptions, only to realize that they have to pay the costs out of pocket.

• Long-Term Care Insurance

Long-term care is an insurance policy that protects you when you cannot take care of yourself. This involves admission to an assisted living facility, nursing home, or any situation that requires a caretaker, usually for more than three months.

• Disability Insurance

Would you be able to get on with life if you had an injury that prevented you from working? Most people wouldn't, and that's where disability insurance comes in. Disability insurance covers incidents that could result in a disability from cancer, a heart attack, or physical injury.

HOW TO GET INSURANCE

For most employed people, it's mandatory for your employer to get you insurance coverage. However, you'll have to pay for it from your pocket if you are not employed. Even though employers pay for your insurance, there's nothing wrong with getting additional private health coverage. This might be useful when the cost of care exceeds the total benefit in your employer's insurance coverage.

If you are a part-time worker, self-employed, or unemployed, get private health insurance, especially if you can't access employer-sponsored insurance coverage. The Affordable Care Act caters to this provision. Before you turn 26, you can still enjoy health insurance under your parent or guardian's policy as a dependent.

An ideal coverage charges affordable insurance premiums for significant benefits in the coverage. You could also opt out of your employer's insurance coverage if you feel it's expensive. However, this might mean missing out on tax credits if your employer's insurance offer meets the legal minimum coverage limits.

IMPORTANT INSURANCE TERMS

Understanding the key terms is the first step to figuring out an insurance contract. Here are some of the most important terms you should know about:

• Premium

This is what you pay the insurer to protect you in the event of a risk, usually billed as a monthly cost. Insurers determine your premiums by assessing various factors about your life, mainly to help them understand the kind of risk they are taking by insuring you.

For example, suppose you have a history of reckless driving. In that case, your premiums will be higher than someone with a spotless driving record because you have a greater probability of raising claims, so you are a greater risk to the insurer.

• Deductibles

This is the amount you pay from your pocket before your insurer can settle your claim, usually discouraging clients from trivial claims. Higher-deductible policies are relatively cheaper and attract fewer trivial claims because customers try to avoid out-of-pocket costs.

Deductibles are paid before the insurance plan can cater to benefits in your coverage. Common costs that might count towards your deductibles include the cost of anesthesia, CAT and MRI scans, lab tests, surgery, and hospitalization bills.

• Co-insurance

This is part of the medical cost you offset once your deductible has been applied. The point is to share the eligible expenses with your insurer to ensure full payment. For example, if the coinsurance in your policy is 15%, you'll have to clear 15% of the cost of treatment, while the insurer pays 85%. Note that you'll still foot the bill for additional costs not included in your policy.

• Copay (Copayment)

This is a flat fee usually paid when filling a prescription or visiting the doctor, meant to offset part of your treatment or medication cost. Some insurance plans have copays, while others use both copays and coinsurance.

- **Policy Limit**

This is the highest amount your insurer can pay toward your claim. For example, let's say your medical insurance coverage has a limit of $100,000. Your insurer can pay no more than $100,000 towards the acceptable medical bills as per your policy document. Higher limits give you more financial room in the event of a claim. These, however, typically attract higher premiums.

5

CREDIT CARDS, CREDIT HISTORY, & CREDIT SCORE

YES IT'S BORING, BUT IT'S IMPORTANT

*C*redit cards are almost synonymous with modern finance. Everyone has one, and some people have more credit cards than they can admit. Credit cards will always remain a divisive subject on personal finances because while they allow you to make purchases easily, they could also be your one-way ticket to financial ruin. After all, a credit card is an expensive loan.

Efficient management is the secret to getting the most value from your credit card. Using your credit card diligently can help you improve your credit score. How can you achieve this? Well, read on and find out more.

CREDIT CARDS AND DEBIT CARDS

A credit card is a loan, so you must pay back the amount spent with interest every month. A debit card, on the other hand, represents your checking account. Therefore, you can think of using a debit card as an account withdrawal.

59

Some debit cards aren't drawn against your checking accounts, such as electronic benefits transfer (EBT) and prepaid debit cards. EBT cards are state or federal agency-issued cards that allow holders to buy stuff with their benefits. Prepaid debit cards are preloaded with cash before use.

Whichever of these two cards you prefer, you should understand their pros and cons to understand how using the card fits into your financial goals. Let's review some of them below:

Credit Card Pros

- Responsible credit card management can help you build a good credit history
- Protection from fraud or card theft under the Electronic Fund Transfer Act, if you report within 48 hours
- Purchase protections like extended warranties in addition to the retailers' offer
- Under the Fair Credit Billing Act, you can dispute erroneous or unauthorized transactions on your card, including items that got lost or damaged in transit

Credit Card Cons

- Credit card mismanagement is one of the leading reasons why many people are currently struggling with debt
- High credit card fees
- Misusing credit cards will erode your credit history

Debit Card Pros

- Considerably low risk of getting into debt
- Fraud protections are similar to credit cards; if you report the misdeed as soon as possible
- Debit cards don't attract the high fees associated with credit cards, like annual fees or cash advance fees

Debit Card Cons

- Since you are not borrowing money from anyone, debit cards won't build your credit
- Don't earn you any rewards like cash backs on some purchases
- Despite the absence of annual fees on the cards, the checking account might be subject to other fees like overdrafts and maintenance fees

CASH OVER CARDS

Using cash instead of cards means spending the amount you have at hand so you stick to your budget. You spend less when using cash than cards because you are consciously aware of the diminishing balance. You think twice about a purchase when you have to pay for it in cash and try to find a cheaper option. Cash buyers have a bargaining advantage. Since vendors don't incur transaction fees or processing delays with cash, it's easier to offer huge discounts on cash purchases.

Cards linked to your account are a hacker's paradise. Identity theft and allied fraud are often associated with stolen cards. You don't have that risk when using cash for your purchases.

Credit cards are one of the key income earners for banks. They are the easiest to access yet most expensive loan facilities extended to customers. So, how do banks make money from them? Simple answer—Interest!

With credit card interest rates averaging 19.33% (some are even higher), banks make a lot of money each time you default on a payment, and your balance spills over to the next month. Apart from interest, credit cards also attract different kinds of fees, which vary across banks.

MAKING MINIMUM PAYMENTS

Minimum payments prevent your account from becoming a deficit, so you don't have to pay penalties for late fees. However, this won't change your loan balance. Remember that the ultimate goal is to clear your credit card debt. Here are some reasons why restricting yourself to minimum payments can be a recipe for disaster:

• **Lengthier Debt Repayment**

Banks generally set minimum payments at very low rates. While these can help you avoid late fees, you remain in their debt for longer because you aren't really making progress on clearing the debt balance.

• **Higher Interest Charges**

Interest on your balance grows with the amount owed. Besides, minimum payments hardly cover the interest charged during the previous month. As long as you still use the card, interest on your balance will keep increasing.

• **Negative Credit Scores**

Your credit utilization ratio increases as your balance increases. High credit utilization damages your credit. Try to keep your utilization ratio to 30% or lower.

TYPES OF CREDIT CARDS

Having considered the pros and cons of using credit cards, if it still fits into your financial strategy, here are some of the major types you'll come across in the market:

- **0% Intro APR credit cards** — These are promotional cards with the 0% offers running for a limited time, generally up to 18 months.
- **Business credit cards** — These are perfect for separating business and personal transactions and can also earn rewards on business expenditures.
- **Cash back credit cards** — These earn you statement credits or cash back.
- **Co-branded credit cards** — These are brand or store-specific cards you can use to redeem rewards on your favorite or supported brands.
- **Rewards credit cards** — These earn you cash back or points on select purchases.
- **Secured credit cards** — These are perfect when you need to rebuild your credit and might be the most accessible cards anyone can be approved for.
- **Store credit cards** — These are offered by major retail outlets, allowing you to shop and clear payments within the store network over time.
- **Student credit cards** — These have relaxed requirements and can be useful for creating a credit history.
- **Travel credit cards** — These earn you travel-related rewards.

Note that the benefits or rewards for using some of these cards could also overlap.

RESPONSIBLE CREDIT CARD USE

Many people get into credit card debt because of misusing their credit cards. This is why most people barely have anything positive to say about credit cards. At the same time, millions of credit card users swear by them and can point to various achievements they couldn't have managed without credit cards. The difference between these two groups of people lies in how they use their credit cards. Below are some valuable tips on responsible credit card usage that you should keep in mind:

1. Read and understand the terms and conditions of the loan agreement.
2. Limit your credit card use to needs, not wants.
3. Make all your payments on time, all the time.
4. Don't exceed 30% of your card limit.
5. Make more than the minimum payments on your balance.
6. Report a lost card, fraudulent transaction, or erroneous entry to your card issuer as soon as you realize it.
7. Keep receipts and use them to review the monthly statement for accuracy.
8. When shopping around for credit cards, try to get a rewards card or one that allows you some rewards, especially at the outlets you frequent.

Even with the points above, the most responsible thing you can do with your credit card, fully aware that this is a loan, is to try and repay the debt in full. Always review the policies to understand the terms and conditions of minimum payments, interest, and fees.

For example, let's look at some scenarios where you owe $8,000 at an interest rate of 15% on a card whose minimum payment is 2% of the balance.

> *At 2%, it will take you more than 30 years to clear the balance, during which you'll have paid in excess of $12,000 in interest payments.*
>
> *At 4%, it will take you more than ten years to clear the balance, during which you'll have paid in excess of $3,000 in interest payments.*
>
> *At 8%, you'll clear the balance in just over five years, during which you'll have paid around $1,500 in interest payments.*

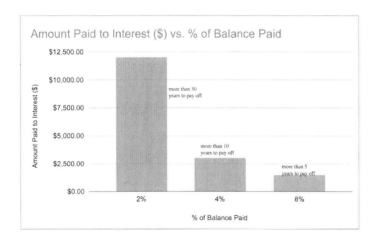

As you can see above, it's always better to try and make more than the minimum expected payment to clear your credit card debt.

Your best option, where possible, is to pay your credit card balances in full. Not only will you avoid expensive interest payments, but you'll also have a better credit score.

* * *

BUILDING CREDIT HISTORY WITH CREDIT CARDS

Lenders assess your creditworthiness before approving your loan requests. This helps them determine whether you can repay the loan. People live different lives, so it's not easy to assess someone's ability at face value. This is where credit history comes in. Lenders review the types of credit accounts, amounts you owe, how long you've been in debt, and so on. Late payments, bankruptcies, or collections will also be evident in the report.

Why is this important? Well, put yourself in the lender's shoes for a moment. Would you be comfortable lending someone money when you can see that they're in no position to pay it back? Of course not. This is why lenders need this information. If your credit isn't good, they can reject your application or consider it at a higher interest rate than someone with better credit. The high-interest rate protects the lender against the possibility that you might default or fail to pay the loan.

There are three possibilities when it comes to your credit history. You could have a good or bad credit history or none at all. Good credit history means you're disciplined and on top of your finances. Your bills are paid on time, and you don't have a lot of debt. This also allows you to lower interest rates on loans or any other credit facility because lenders trust your repayment ability.

Bad credit history is a sign of financial indiscipline and irresponsibility. You are always behind on bills, deep in debt, or fund most of your purchases with credit. You might also have been a victim of repossession, foreclosure, or filed for bankruptcy. Lenders avoid you at first glance at your credit history and reject your applications. Those willing to take chances with you will ask for security deposits or charge higher interest.

You could also have no credit history if you've never been in a position to pay bills or ask for a loan. College students and young adults leaving their parents' nest usually fall into this category. With nothing to go on, lenders or even landlords don't know anything about your ability to honor your financial obligations, so they'd be equally hesitant to extend you their services as they would to someone with a bad credit history. No one likes to be the guinea pig in your financial journey.

Despite being one of the leading reasons many people have terrible credit, a credit card can be an equally valuable tool for building your credit back up. It's all about disciplined and responsible usage. While at it, try to restrict your purchases to a small percentage of your credit limit to maintain a low utilization rate.

If you don't have a credit card, sign up for one, or if you can't get one because of bad or no credit history, get a secured credit card or student credit card, or ask someone to add you as an authorized user on their card. As an authorized user, the primary account holder, for example, your parents, can set limits on your credit card because they bear primary responsibility for the card.

Below are other methods you can use to build credit if you don't have a credit card, are having a difficult time getting one, or simply don't want one:

- **Auto Loans**

Car loans are secured by the vehicle you purchase, so lenders consider them less risky than traditional unsecured loans. Lenders also report auto loan payments to credit bureaus, so your payments won't be in vain.

• Federal Student Loans

These loans are great for students, especially since most don't need a credit history for approval. They will show up on your credit report, so apply for one if you are certain you can pay it back.

• Personal Loans

If you don't mind the high-interest rates, some lenders can allow you unsecured personal loans even if you don't have a credit history. With a co-signer on a loan, you might even be able to get lower interest rates.

• Rent

Pay rent on time, even if your landlord doesn't submit rent information to credit bureaus. It's a good practice in financial responsibility, and where it counts, it might be one of the simplest ways to build your credit history.

• Certificate of Deposit (CD) Loans

These follow a similar approach to credit builder loans and can also be issued by banks. The loan is charged against the balance in your CD account. Since the loan is secured by your savings, their interest rates are usually lower. Before you sign up, however, make sure your bank reports these transactions to the major credit bureaus.

• Credit Builder Loans

These are usually offered by credit unions and other smaller financial institutions where you borrow a small amount of money and pay it back. The money is deposited into a savings account, where it stays until you pay off the loan.

* * *

CREDIT SCORES

Credit scores help lenders determine your creditworthiness based on a historical record of your financial activity. Here is some of the historical information that determines your credit score:

- Your history of bill payments
- Type and number of loan accounts
- How long you've held the loan accounts
- Any unpaid debt
- Applications for loans and other credit facilities
- If you have credit, how much of it are you using?
- Whether you've ever been foreclosed, had any account in collection, or been declared bankrupt

Credit reporting bureaus have different approaches for determining your credit score, but they generally revolve around the factors above.

Credit scores are assigned in the range of 300 to 850, with anything above 670 considered a good credit score on the Fair Isaac Company (FICO) scoring model for measuring consumer credit risk. As your score increases, you become a desirable borrower to lenders. The FICO scoring model is as follows:

300 - 579 (Poor)
580 - 669 (Fair)

670 - 739 (Good)
740 - 799 (Very Good)
800 - 850 (Exceptional)

Some employers also run credit checks to help them understand your level of financial discipline and responsibility, so your credit score might cost you a promotion or a job.

Credit Score Determinants

You should always make an effort to improve your credit score. Here are the five important factors that determine your credit score:

1. **Payment History** — Timely payments are good for your credit score. Missed payments, bankruptcy, or having an account in collections will negatively affect your credit score.
2. **Duration of Credit** — This is based on the average age of your open credit accounts, from the oldest to the newest.
3. **Credit Use** — This depends on your credit limit, the total amount you owe, and the number of open credit accounts you have.
4. **Credit Mix** — This assessment depends on the type of credit accounts you have and is based on revolving accounts like credit cards and installment accounts like mortgages and car loans. The idea here is to establish whether you can comfortably manage both.
5. **Recent Credit Activity** — The emphasis here is on whether you've opened or applied for a new line of credit recently.

Check your credit score to understand your current financial standing. Most financial institutions allow you at least one free credit score request annually. You could also request a credit score from the major reporting agencies: TransUnion, Equifax, and Experian.

Improving Your Credit Score

Once you have your credit score, take steps to improve it or maintain it if you have outstanding credit. Here are some important tips to guide you through this:

- Never apply for credit when you don't need it. Every new application could result in a hard inquiry. Hard inquiries hurt your scores because they create the impression that you are hard-pressed for cash.
- Ensure your accounts are reporting to credit bureaus. If they don't, you'll miss the opportunity to improve your credit rating, despite your financial discipline.
- Never exceed your credit utilization rate. Similar to the first point, exceeding this limit creates the impression that you cannot manage your life without debt.
- Do not close your old credit accounts because this reduces your credit score.
- Never miss a payment. Make at least the minimum payment required if things are rough.

Apart from the points above, maintain a primary residence or place of employment for at least two years. This helps lenders establish stability in your life and that they can physically trace you if needed. Finally, review the report frequently to identify errors, omissions, or fraudulent entries and report them to the relevant agencies or authorities immediately.

Hard vs. Soft Inquiries

An inquiry is a process where lenders check your credit score in your application to learn about your financial responsibility and discipline from historical records of your financial activity.

Hard inquiries occur for lending purposes, for example, when applying for a credit card, loan, or mortgage, usually with your permission. Soft inquiries are checks into your credit as part of a background check, usually without your consent. Checking your own credit scores counts as a soft inquiry.

The main difference between these two is that while hard inquiries affect your credit score, soft inquiries won't. The only challenge is that some credit checks can show up as either, so it's not easy to tell how that will go. Examples include phone, internet, cable, and utility service provider checks. You can, however, ask these providers how their checks are classified beforehand.

GETTING A STUDENT CREDIT CARD WITH NO CREDIT

The student credit card is one of the easiest you can qualify for since you don't have a credit history. It's a good way to learn financial responsibility, setting you up for good credit early in life. Let's go through some simple steps on how to get this credit card:

Step #1: Review your credit report

Check your reports for any inaccurate or erroneous entries that could impede your chances of a successful application.

Step #2: Window shopping

There are many student cards in the market, so take your time and compare different options. Consider the potential rewards, fees, and APR on the card.

Step #3: Eligibility

Check the card issuer's eligibility terms to see if you qualify or not. Generally, you must have a Social Security number, be a college student of at least 18 years old, and have either a co-signer on the card or a source of income.

Step #4: Proof of eligibility

Provide the documents necessary to prove your eligibility, for example, proof of college enrollment (transcripts or your acceptance letter) or proof of income (pay stubs or W-2 tax forms).

Step #5: Co-signers

Where necessary, you can get a relative, friend, or parent to co-sign your application forms if you don't have sufficient income or are under 21.

Step #6: Apply

For online applications, you usually get feedback in minutes. A delayed response might mean further review of your application. However, the card is mailed to you as soon as the approval is in. Assuming your application is rejected, card issuers generally write you a letter explaining their reasons (the adverse action notice). This can be an eye-opener, as it details what you can do to improve your chances on the next application.

Applying for a student credit card ushers you into the world of financial responsibility. Every decision involving your card from this day onwards will greatly influence future financial decisions in your life. Exercise restraint and think twice before making significant financial purchases or commitments against your card.

6

THE SMART SHOPPER

WHY PAY MORE?

*S*hopping—we do it all the time. There's always
something to be bought at home, whether it's food,
some clothes, a new smartphone, a new car, or even a new
house. The essence of money in the economy is to keep it in
circulation. Shopping is one of the most common ways of
achieving that. The challenge that most of us experience is
that we don't know how to spend our money right.

> *"Too many people spend money they haven't earned to buy things*
> *they don't want, to impress people that they don't like."*
> —*Will Rogers*

The quote above sums up what we might refer to as
unhealthy spending habits. The most important question
therefore is, are you that person? And if so, what are you
doing about it?

No one likes to admit they paid too much for something or
were ripped off on a purchase. These are hard lessons many
people keep to themselves and probably never visit the same

store in the future. You've probably been in this position a few times already, right?

It's funny that in a shopping ecosystem where freebies, discounts, offers, sales, and all kinds of deals exist, people still spend more than they should. The truth is that some of these irresistible offers, which sound too good to be true, usually are. You can easily figure this out through smart shopping. What's the difference between an intelligent shopper and the average shopper? Well, let's briefly discuss some definitive traits of a smart shopper:

• **Proactive Shopper**

Smart shoppers have email subscriptions and app notifications that alert them to updates from their favorite stores. Thus, they are always in the know, well ahead of other shoppers who find out about deals and offers through word of mouth or by surprise when they are out shopping and end up spending on things they never planned for.

• **Disciplined Shopping**

Smart shopping and discipline go hand in hand. You must have a budget and stick to it. Prioritize the household needs, like stocking the pantry over splurging on trendy clothes. More importantly, you won't find an intelligent shopper scouring the internet for deals every other week. They have their priorities figured out and probably shop once a month.

• **Economic Buys**

As a smart shopper, you understand that most bargains trick you into buying more than you need. This is hoarding, driven by the scarcity mentality that the bargain might end soon. Smart shoppers don't do that. They only buy what they need, whether there's a discount offer or not.

- **Deal or Outright Scam?**

A smart shopper knows that most promotional deals are either a rip-off, a ploy to trick them into signing up for an unnecessary payment plan, or get them into spending over their budget. The secret is to think long-term. If you consider the interest rates and other hidden charges stores never disclose openly, you might realize that the 'bargains' aren't as discounted as they'd want you to believe.

- **Conscious Shoppers**

Besides considerable savings in their pockets, smart shoppers are keen on saving the environment. From reusable shopping bags to space-saving boxes, smart shoppers are also smart packagers, so retail outlets are now inclined to offer eco-friendly packaging solutions.

One thing stands out from the traits above—awareness. Smart shoppers don't just go with the flow. They know what they want, what to pay for it, and when to walk away from it.

THE MAKINGS OF A SMART SHOPPER

We have already seen what it takes to consider yourself a smart shopper, so let's look at practical tips to help you start shopping smart TODAY!

1. Credit Card Management

Smart shoppers use their credit cards wisely. Apart from avoiding unnecessary purchases, always try to find cashback reward providers like Discover so that you can earn money on your card with some purchases. You must always clear your credit card balances. Credit cards are the easiest way to slide into debt, so use yours cautiously.

2. Budget-Conscious Shopping

Smart shopping and budgeting go hand in hand. Other than ensuring you don't overspend, budgets also help you remember the important stuff, thus meeting your needs within your income limits.

3. Price Comparisons

Always compare prices, especially when drawing up your shopping list from your budget. Even though shopping online is much easier, you can also compare prices in local stores to get a great deal.

4. Bulk Purchases

It's no secret that you can save so much through bulk shopping, especially at wholesale outlets. However, you must also research well to get the best per-item value for your money. Bulk shopping is ideal, especially for non-perishable items.

5. Impulse Buying

Stop impulse buying right away. If you feel so pressed to buy something that wasn't on your list, note it down and forget about it for a while. More often, whether it was a necessary purchase or not will become apparent soon enough.

6. Second-Hand Stores

You don't always have to buy new products. There are many products you can purchase from second-hand stores at significant discounts and still enjoy as much utility and value from them as you'd have from the new products.

7. Clearance Sale

It doesn't hurt to wait for a clearance sale. If you frequent certain stores, you'll probably know some of the items listed on clearance sales. This is an excellent opportunity to score incredible discounts.

8. Seasonal Shopping

Seasonal products generally have different prices throughout the year, usually because of changes in demand. For example, most Christmas products will be pricey in December because everyone's rushing to buy them. You can get some of them at steep discounts earlier in the year. At the same time, you could also get great seasonal discounts during the holidays, especially on gadgets and clothes.

9. Cashbacks and Coupons

Cashback websites like Rakuten (formerly Ebates) and coupons exist so that you can take advantage of them. They earn through referrals and advertising revenue, which they, in turn, share with customers who buy from partner merchants.

You can also get rebates on household purchases, groceries, and other everyday purchases through money-saving apps like Ibotta or market research companies like Receipt Hog.

Here's something you probably didn't know—Rakuten is Japanese for optimism!

The lesson here is that even though you'll have to buy things from time to time, what sets a smart shopper apart from every other shopper is how you approach it. Ideally, smart shoppers always try to get more value for their money.

Thus, the next time you're considering splurging on a new $1,000 phone, take a moment and think about the finer details. Say you earn $20 an hour. You'll have to work 50 hours to afford the new phone without borrowing money. Remember that this is 50 hours where all your income goes toward buying the phone. You haven't factored in your bills and other pressing commitments. With this approach, you might reconsider whether working 50 hours for a new phone is worth it, especially when you have a phone that still serves you well.

SPEND SMART WITH UNIT PRICING

Still, to get more value for your money, unit pricing is one of the smartest strategies you can implement. Manufacturers and stores generally sell products in a variety of sizes. By default, we assume that this is meant to meet the needs of different customers. While this might be true, it could also be a smart way to trick you into paying more for less value. Well, you can beat them at their game through unit pricing.

Unit pricing means comparing similar products to determine which one gets you the best deal for your money. This helps you get the actual cost of a single item in a package. Let's explain this with some examples:

Let's say you've run out of cat food. A 20-pound bag goes for $14.29, while a 15-pound bag goes for $11.49.

To get the unit price per pound, you divide the overall price by the label weight.

In this case, you are getting cat food at $0.71 a pound for the 20-pound bag or $0.77 a pound for the 15-pound bag. Even though the price is higher, buying the 20-pound bag gets you more value.

To determine the unit price, you can do the same for items sold in bales, dozens, and other quantities.

Nutritional labels on food products can also help you make a smart choice. For example, most foods include the recommended serving size. Say you are buying some canned food and have to choose between two cans with the following info:

Can 1: 10 recommended servings at $2.71
Can 2: 15 recommended servings at $4.55

Using the earlier approach, you are choosing between $0.27 per serving in Can 1 and $0.30 per serving in Can 2.

In this case, even though Can 2 gives you more servings, you get more value for money in Can 1.

The lesson here is that bigger doesn't always translate to more savings. However, stores sometimes offer discounts on larger products. Either way, you should still use unit pricing on the discounted price to make sure you are not being duped.

COST PER WEAR

You can also apply the concept of unit pricing to the clothes you buy. In this case, we'll interpret it as cost per wear. Cost per wear helps you understand the actual utility value you get from your clothes by comparing the price against the number of times you'll wear them. At a glance, you can tell that you get more value from clothes you'll wear several times than those you'll only wear once.

Cost per wear is determined by dividing the price of the clothes by the number of times you wore them or the number of times you intend to wear them.

Let's say you spent $50 on a branded shirt and wore it 90 times. The cost per wear for the shirt will be 50 ÷ 90 = $0.55. If you only wore the shirt five times, the cost per wear will be 50 ÷ 5 = $10.

Now, while the example above gives us the cost per wear for the shirt, it doesn't tell us anything about whether the shirt is affordable or not. To get that, we'd have to compare two or more items.

For example, if you wore the shirt 50 times, the cost per wear would be $1, similar to buying a $200 shirt and wearing it 200 times. In this case, we can assume that for 200 wears, the shirt must be quite durable so that the quality could justify the price. However, on price alone, this is like comparing apples to oranges.

Cost per wear can be useful when comparing items of the same price. For example, the $50 shirt you can wear 90 times, against a $50 shirt you can wear 20 times. The cost per wear for the second shirt will be 50 ÷ 20 = $2.5. The first shirt is a more economical purchase than the second. Of course, whichever option you choose, it's always advisable to go for better quality.

QUALITY OVER QUANTITY

Many people make purchase decisions based on pricing. The problem here is that this only factors in the quantity. The amount often doesn't tell you much about the quality, yet it's the most important thing in a purchase. Going for quality purchases, from clothes to food and other items, generally gives you more value than quantity. Here are some reasons why you should always focus on quality purchases instead of overwhelming quantity:

• Think Long-Term

Quality guarantees you affordability for a long time. Even if the price is relatively higher, quality purchases save you more money because they last longer. You must be careful, however, because some premium labels that cost considerably higher don't necessarily guarantee quality. At the same time, since you don't need to replace the purchased item frequently, buying quality is cost-effective, considering the time and energy invested in the purchase.

• Sustainability

We generally take better care of quality purchases than relatively poorer quality items. With proper care, they last longer in our homes instead of ending up in landfills. In the long run, quality purchases are friendlier to the environment.

Still, on sustainability, it's better to have fewer good-quality items than many poor-quality items. Think in terms of care and maintenance, for example. It's more overwhelming and stressful to keep replacing or fixing poor-quality products. These are valuable time and resources which you could spend doing something productive.

• Greater Satisfaction

Let's use the example of healthy organic food here. A clean, healthy, balanced diet is good for your health. You sleep better, your body metabolism is awesome, and you rarely fall sick, so you don't frequent the hospital. Overall, you live a satisfying life.

On the other hand, you could get so much junk food for a fraction of the amount you spend on healthy food, but the long-term implications have far-reaching effects beyond immediate satiety. You are looking at the risk of lifestyle diseases that shorten your lifespan—and spending more time and money in the hospital.

- **Consciousness**

When you buy quality over quantity, you become more aware of the purchases. You don't just buy something because it's available or on offer. Your purchases are carefully thought over and are mostly seen as investments. Such thoughtfulness makes you more conscious about spending your money and your duty of care to yourself. In a way, you can think of quality purchases as self-love. You buy quality products because you know you deserve the best.

Ultimately, the issue of quality vs. quantity transcends purchases and applies to most aspects of your life. From social interactions and relationships to books and vacations, quality will always add more value to your life than quantity.

SMART SHOPPING AND ONLINE RETAIL

Widespread access to the internet has sped up the online retail revolution, transforming how we shop and interact with our favorite brands. As stores try to capitalize on the ease of accessing their customers, it's even more essential to become smarter in how you go about shopping. Without this, you could easily fall prey to marketing gimmicks and spend your money carelessly.

Ultimately, a smart shopper will always look for money-saving opportunities. Below are some valuable tips you can implement when shopping online that will help you save more money:

- **Understand Dynamic Pricing**

Retailers generally track and try to capitalize on consumer habits like spending patterns, online engagements, and browsing history. With this information, they can adjust their prices to profitable margins according to real-time changes in supply and demand.

You've probably experienced this before, especially when booking flights, where flight prices increase shortly after you've looked them up but didn't complete the booking. The assumption here is usually that you must be seriously considering the purchase to view the listing more than once, hence the price increase.

This uncanny trick might seem like a scam, but it is a legal pricing strategy. Falling prey to it means spending more than you should. You can avoid this by shopping online using a VPN or incognito mode, so retailers cannot track your activities.

On the same note, clear your browsing history and cookies before shopping to dupe online algorithms into thinking you are a new customer. Finally, use tools like Google Shopping to compare prices and get the best deals.

- **Discount Shopping**

Companies like Ibotta and Rakuten (formerly Ebates) have strategic partnerships with popular brands, allowing you to earn back a percentage of your money while shopping online or in-store. From booking a vacation for your family to shopping for groceries, there are endless opportunities to earn back some of your money from various retail outlets online.

- **Redeemable Shopping Points**

You can also earn points every time you shop online through MyPoints. These redeemable points can be used to pay for stuff or withdraw into your PayPal wallet. While the approach is almost similar to Rakuten's cashback concept, the difference here is that apart from shopping, you can also earn points from playing video games, taking surveys, or watching videos.

Online shopping can be a confusing maze that costs too much money or an amazing experience. It all depends on how you approach it. Honey, for example, is an extension that automatically finds you the best coupons to help you save the most. Try the tips we've discussed herein from time to time, and you'll be surprised at how much more money you can save from your budget.

7

BANKS, INTEREST, AND LOANS

THE SOONER YOU'RE EDUCATED ABOUT THEM, THE BETTER OFF YOU'LL BE

*B*anks are financial institutions whose mandate under their license includes receiving customer deposits, issuing loans, managing investments, and engaging in the purchase and sale of money. Banks also engage in other activities like insurance and mortgaging. However, at the end of the day, banks are involved in almost every other financial activity you can think of.

Banks have been in the headlines for all the wrong reasons. Remember the 2008 financial crisis? Well, banks were at the center of it. In its wake, many people were left jobless, companies folded, and many homeowners lost their homes.

From time to time, bank customers complain about fraudulent charges, activities, and scams on their accounts. Online banking, for example, made it easier for customers to use their money as they please. On the flip side, this also opened avenues for criminals to hack online accounts and wipe them clean. Cases of identity theft are almost always linked to fraudulent bank activity.

Clearly, banks aren't necessarily the good guys, right? The list of ills attributed to banks could be endless, but aren't we all just as imperfect as they are? Despite these challenges, banks have existed in different forms for centuries because they are an integral part of our lives, especially our economy. Here are some good reasons why you should use a bank:

- **Utmost Security**

Banks offer better security for your wealth than anyone else. From individuals to companies and even governments, money is safer in a bank's custody. Besides, all banks take insurance policies to protect their customers' wealth. Thus, you can be certain of a fallback plan if the bank ever collapses or is robbed.

- **Economic Champion**

Banks support the economy by lending to individuals, small businesses, and large corporations alike, so everyone can pursue their goals, creating more jobs in the process.

- **Accessibility of Money**

Banks manage a large pool of money from which we can borrow for different reasons. Deposits and other sources of income make it easier for banks to support our dreams through loans. Banks have many other roles, suitable for individuals, small and large businesses, and governments alike. As you grow older and your financial needs evolve, so will your interaction with banks, opening your world to new experiences in banking.

CHOOSING THE RIGHT BANK

The debate of banks vs. credit unions will always come up in your search for a reliable financial partner. Each institution ensures safe custody of your money and stands with you every step of your financial journey. Let's compare some of their distinct features to help you make the right decision.

● **Membership and Ownership**

Banks are investor-owned businesses that are operated for profit. Credit unions, on the other hand, are member-owned non-profit businesses. While banks are driven by their profit-making obligation to investors, credit unions serve the vested interests of their members, for example, offering high interest on savings and low interest on loans.

Under their ownership models, bank customers do not have voting rights on matters concerning the bank. Their interest as customers ends at the transactional nature of their contract with the bank. On the other hand, credit union customers are also members, so they have a say in how the institution operates.

● **Business Products**

Banks have a variety of banking products for both commercial and personal needs. This includes investment vehicles like IRAs, forex, and money market products. On the other hand, credit unions have a limited product range, particularly on the commercial front. Their products are primarily traditional banking facilities like credit cards, savings, and checking accounts.

● **Interest Rates**

Credit unions offer famously low-interest rates on loans and other credit facilities like mortgages compared to banks. Their savings accounts also provide much better yields than you'll get from banks. Hands down, banks have nothing on credit unions regarding interest rates. Even so, banks offer some competitive rates among themselves, so if you choose the bank way, always research the market for the best terms.

• Fees

Like interest rates, banks charge the highest fees compared to credit unions since they are in the profit-making business. So high are their fees that, in most cases, freebies come with strings attached. For example, a free checking account could have mandatory minimum balances. Most credit unions have checking accounts without monthly service fees. Or minimum balance requirements. Credit unions also tend to lower fees for other activities like bounced checks.

• Technological Advancements

Banks are more tech-savvy than credit unions. Their financial muscle gives them the advantage of tapping into the top technological talent in the industry. This is why it's easier for banks to introduce or refine tech products like mobile and online banking and a wider ATM network. Many credit unions offer similar products, but they might not be at par with banks in efficiency or quality because of their limited tech budget.

Whichever of these two you choose, always remember that the goal is to meet your financial needs. Either way, your money will always be safe in banks and credit unions. The National Credit Union Administration (NCUA) for credit unions, and the Federal Deposit Insurance Corporation (FDIC) for banks, insure customer accounts up to $250,000. Beyond this amount, you can consult the respective account managers for advice on your account safety.

INTERNET BANKING

Most people are drawn to internet banking by the convenience of easy access. This, however, doesn't mean it's always a smooth experience. For example, you cannot build personal relationships with bank staff because everything is done online. If anything, even the customer support services these days are mostly run by artificial intelligence bots.

Without the personal touch, it's difficult to address certain issues that would generally be easier if you physically visited the bank and spoke to an account manager. You can imagine the frustration of having problems with an international transaction.

Internet banking services are also limited. For example, you probably won't be able to get preferred interest rates because, let's face it, whom will you negotiate with? On top of that, internet banking franchises don't have independent ATMs, so you'll mainly be using ATM networks like Cirrus.

Despite these challenges, internet banking is here to stay. Banks are aware that their customers enjoy the convenience and are increasingly enhancing the online banking experience. This, coupled with relatively lower fees and better rates, has more customers weighing their options in favor of internet banking. Ultimately, it is still a bank, so you enjoy similar protections like FDIC insurance.

* * *

INTEREST AND INTEREST RATES

Interest is the cost of using money. For savings accounts, this is the cost banks pay you for using your deposits, while for loans, it is the cost you pay for borrowing the bank's money. Let's explain this with an example.

Say you borrowed $1,000 at a simple interest rate of 5% for three years. The parameters of this loan are as follows:

Principal amount borrowed = $1,000
Rate of interest = 5%
Duration of the loan = 3 years
The total interest earned = Principal amount x Rate
   of interest x Duration of the loan
= $1,000 x 5% x 3
= $150

At the end of the loan period, you'll pay back a total of $1,150, where $1,000 is the original amount you borrowed (principal), and $150 is the total interest (the total cost of borrowing $1,000).

For most banking products like credit cards, interest is usually referred to as the annual percentage rate (APR). The APR is, in some cases, bundled with other costs relevant to the loan, making it higher than the base interest rate. For this reason, it's always advisable to consider both the APR and base interest rate to understand the true cost of credit.

The true APR of a loan facility is derived as follows:

Step #1: Total interest + Loan fees
Step #2: (Answer in Step 1) ÷ Loan amount
Step #3: (Answer in Step 2) ÷ Duration to pay the
   loan, in days
Step #4: (Answer in Step 3) x 365 x 100

Using our earlier example, but with a loan administration fee of $100, our APR will be as follows:

Step #1: $150 + $100 = $250
Step #2: $250 ÷ $1,000 = 0.25
Step #3: 0.25 ÷ 1095 = 0.00022831
Step #4: 0.00022831 x 365 x 100
APR = 8.33%

In this case, you'll realize that at 8.33%, the APR is considerably higher than the original interest rate of 5% because it factored in additional costs.

There are other kinds of interest rates you might come across in different banking products other than APR. Here are some of the common ones:

- **Fixed Interest** — This interest rate never changes throughout the term of the contract, so both parties to the contract are aware of the costs involved.
- **Variable Interest** — These interest rates fluctuate through the contract terms in response to changes in the underlying terms.
- **Discount Rate** – This is the rate at which banks and other financial institutions borrow money from the Federal Reserve. Banks can use this position to shore up liquidity and avert a crisis.
- **Prime Rate** – This is a special rate that banks offer certain customers, usually large business clients, because of their creditworthiness. It's also the basic rate that banks use to set the market rate for different products.
- **Simple Interest** – This is the interest we used in the first example that gave us a total interest of $150.

- **Compound Interest** – Interest amount increases annually by earning on interest already earned. The principal interest in subsequent years will be the previous period's principal amount, plus the interest earned on it.

HOW DO I EARN INTEREST?

Ever noticed how banks charge insane interest rates when you ask for a loan, but the interest they pay you to use your money in your savings account is laughable? This is one of the ways they exploit you. Besides, if you factor in the cost of inflation, your money loses value in your savings account. Instead of losing money to banks, here are some clever ways to earn better interest without assuming unnecessary risk:

- **Certificate of Deposit** – Despite their withdrawal restrictions, these generally have better interest rates than the average savings accounts.
- **Certificate of Deposit Ladders** – A CD ladder means spacing your CDs within regular intervals. For example, opening 12 CDs maturing precisely one month from the next, for a year. This way, after a year, you'll be cashing out high-interest savings every month.
- **Introductory Offers** – Pay attention to introductory offers when banks launch new products. You could get some decent interest savings through these.
- **High-Interest Savings Account** – The rates on these savings accounts are usually higher than for standard savings accounts.
- **Treasury Bonds** – If you won't need the money for a while, buy bonds instead of putting it in a savings account.

- **Credit Unions** – Credit unions offer better interest rates than banks so that you can open a savings account with them instead of a bank.
- **Money Markets** – If you don't mind the fees, you could invest that money in a money market fund, whose interests could even be higher than what you'd get from high-yield savings accounts.

Even though each option above can earn you better interest than a traditional savings account, the best choice will depend on the level of risk you can take and your personal financial goals.

CERTIFICATE OF DEPOSIT (CD) VS. SAVINGS ACCOUNT

CDs are an excellent opportunity to supplement your savings plan because of the fixed returns. You are aware of the amount of interest you'll earn through the term of the CD. This makes them a good investment for the money you won't need in a while. However, if you'd wish to access the money from time to time, you'd be better off keeping it in a savings account.

Even though some banks waived the requirement, you must place a minimum deposit with most banks to open a CD, which usually ranges from $50 to $1,000, or higher, depending on the bank. Note that once you open the CD, you cannot add or withdraw money from the account until its term expires without attracting a penalty.

Savings accounts, on the other hand, are generally hassle-free. An open minimum deposit means you are free to deposit whatever amount you wish to activate the account, though many banks don't require a minimum deposit.

Unlike CDs, you can access your money in a savings account all the time. You can equally deposit and withdraw from it whenever necessary without incurring penalties.

Note, however, that bank withdrawal limits encourage a savings culture. Limits vary in every bank, so it's wise to understand the withdrawal terms so you don't end up in a situation where you need money but cannot withdraw it from your bank. Besides, if you exceed the bank's withdrawal limit, the bank could convert your savings account into a checking account, whose charges and fees might not be favorable.

* * *

LOANS

A loan is any money you borrow from someone, a group of people, or an institution to be paid back with interest at an agreed-upon date. Loans are structured as follows:

- **Principal amount** – This is the amount you receive from the lender.
- **Interest** – This is the loan cost, which you will pay back together with the principal amount.
- **Installment payments** – These are regular fixed payments made towards clearing the loan.
- **Term of the loan** – This is the duration of time within which you should have repaid the loan in full.

Understanding these terms should help you establish whether the loan is affordable and suitable for your needs.

Loans are broadly classified as secured and unsecured loans. A secured loan is backed by an asset, usually of a higher value than the loan, which is forfeited to the lender if you can't pay the loan. An unsecured loan isn't backed by any asset but is issued against proof that you can pay it back. Proof could be your paycheck, a letter of employment, or a history of transactions in your account.

Secured loans have lower interest rates than unsecured loans because lenders have a fallback plan if you default. There's more risk to the lender in an unsecured loan, hence the higher interest rates.

Loans can also be classified as revolving or term loans. A revolving loan is a flexible loan where you can borrow, repay the loan, and re-borrow. On the other hand, term loans must be cleared within the duration of the loan. A good example of an unsecured revolving loan is a credit card, while a car loan qualifies as a secured term loan.

ADVANTAGES AND DISADVANTAGES OF A PERSONAL LOAN

You can qualify for a personal loan in most banks with good credit. Before you apply, weigh your options to understand what you are getting yourself into. Let's look at some of the pros and cons of loans below:

- **Fast approval** – As long as you meet the qualification criteria, personal loans have fast approval times, which is awesome, especially for emergencies.
- **Lump sum payments** – You'll receive the entire amount approved, making it easier to attend to your needs, especially for large purchases.
- **Collateral requirements** – You won't need collateral to guarantee your loan. However, failure to pay the loan will affect your credit negatively.

- **Flexibility** – You can use a personal loan for whatever reason you need to. This is different from auto loans, which are strictly for buying a car.
- **Affordable Interest** – Personal loans usually have lower interest rates. At the time of this publication, they averaged 10.28% compared to 16.80% for credit cards.
- **Management** – You can take a substantial personal loan to consolidate debt. A single-interest payment is easier to handle than multiple interest payments on different debts.
- **Reasonable Payment Terms** – You can negotiate terms to a manageable amount every month. However, a lengthier duration will mean more interest payments.

Despite the benefits above, personal loans might not always be the solution to your needs all the time. Here are some potential challenges you might experience with these loans:

- **Eligibility Barriers** – Lenders have strict eligibility criteria to protect themselves from the risk of customer default.
- **Penalties and Fees** – Fees and penalties on personal loans could make them more expensive in the long run, especially if you have bad credit.
- **Debt Burden** – While personal loans can be helpful to consolidate debt, they increase your debt burden without addressing the underlying reasons why you are in debt.
- **Strict Terms** – You must clear your personal loan by the end of the loan term. Credit cards, however, allow you smaller, manageable payments without a deadline.

- **Budget Problems** – Additional monthly payments on personal loans could strain your budget, resulting in more financial problems down the line.

FACTORS THAT DETERMINE YOUR LOAN INTEREST

You've probably noticed that interest rates vary from one lender to the next. This is usually because, as a measure of the risk of lending you money, lenders consider different factors, hence these differences. Have you ever wondered how lenders arrive at this decision? Well, here are some of the factors that lenders consider when setting interest rates for your loans:

1. **Credit History** – You'll always get a reasonable rate with a good credit history showing a financially responsible person.
2. Credit Score – Higher credit scores get you lower interest rates.
3. **Income Status** – Your employment status informs lenders of your ability to repay the loan.
4. **Type of Loan** – Interest rates vary according to the type of loan.
5. **Loan Duration** – You generally get better rates with a shorter payment duration.
6. **Loan Amount** – Interest rates are generally higher for smaller loans, for example, less than $100,000.
7. **Payment Frequency** – Interest will also depend on your preferred payment frequency, for example, monthly or annually.
8. **Type of Property** – Lenders consider the risk in the property for which you need the loan. A commercial farm, for example, is riskier than a residential house.

9. **Documentation** – The more documents you can provide to prove your ability to pay the loan, the higher your chances of getting a better interest rate.
10. **Co-borrowers** – Lenders will consider the credit position of everyone else on the loan when setting interest rates.
11. **Debt Ratio** – Lenders compare your overall monthly debt obligation against your monthly income to ensure they don't burden you with more debt than you can handle.
12. **Loan to Value (LTV)** – Lenders prefer a lower LTV, the portion of the borrowed amount that goes to buying the property in question.
13. **Combined Loan to Value (CLTV)** - This ratio considers the loan you've requested, plus any other loans you might be servicing when setting your interest rates.

The points above are the most important factors lenders consider when setting interest rates. However, they are not the only ones. Below are other additional factors that can influence their decision:

1. **Occupancy** – Investment and rental properties generally attract higher rates.
2. **Escrow** – Lenders who use escrows for transaction costs like insurance and taxes can charge higher interests if you don't escrow, as it increases your risk potential.
3. **Residency** — You get lower rates for a primary residence than a second home.
4. **Relocation** — Your employment status determines whether the residence is primary or secondary, and interest rates apply as above.

5. **Employment Status** — A history of stable employment gives you better interest rates.
6. **Gifts** — You can reduce your loan amount with gifts from friends and family members, effectively reducing your interest rate.
7. **Collateral** — For secured loans, you can get better interest rates with a higher down payment.
8. **Asset Seasoning** — Some lenders can consider how long you've owned certain assets when determining your interest rate.
9. **Housing Ratio** — This is the percentage of your pre-tax income that goes to your housing expenses. Ratios lower than 28% can get you better interest rates.
10. **Property Improvements** — Property value is affected by the need for improvements. Lower LTVs generally get you better interest rates.
11. **Refinancing** — Refinancing with the aim of getting a cash-out increases your LTV.
12. **Closing Date** — You get better rates when you lock in an interest rate for a longer period before the closing date.
13. **Seller Contributions** — For property purchases, if your seller can contribute to the closing costs, you'll have more money for a down payment on the property, giving you a better argument for lower interest rates.

Discussing some of these factors with your lender when asking for a loan can give you a better chance of negotiating interest rates in your favor.

WHEN TO ASK FOR A LOAN

When you need a personal loan, you are so preoccupied with solving the problem at hand that you forget to check for affordable alternatives. Some common reasons why a personal loan might suffice include:

- You need financial support for a short time.
- You don't have collateral for a secured loan, so this is the most affordable option you have.
- To finance a huge financial obligation, like a home improvement.
- To clear high-interest debts or consolidate your debt.
- Your credit card limits can't sustain your immediate needs.
- You can't qualify for a low-interest credit card.
- To finance a significant event in life, like a wedding.
- To improve your credit score with timely payments.

The most important thing about asking for a loan is ensuring you can afford to pay it back. Remember that personal loans might be easy to qualify for, but they could also land you in debt.

HOW TO GET A PERSONAL LOAN

Always research the market for the best rates and whether the terms align with your personal finance needs. Talk to bank staff to learn more about the requirements, then prepare the necessary documents. Here are some of the items you'll need for this application:

- Personal identification documents
- Proof of residence

- Employer information
- Proof of income

Once you have all these documents ready, the next step is to meet the technical requirements. The steps below will guide you accordingly:

Step #1: Do the Math

Always research the market for the best rates and whether the terms align with your personal finance needs. Talk to bank staff to learn more about the requirements, then prepare the necessary documents. Here are some of the items you'll need for this application:

Step #2: Credit Checks

Lenders will consider your credit score, among other factors. Generally, a credit score above 580 should guarantee you favorable interest rates.

Step #3: Weigh Your Options

You should get better interest rates with some collateral where necessary. If your credit isn't great, a co-signer with good credit can help you get approved for a decent rate.

Step #4: Type of Loan

Some lenders strictly use the loan only for its intended purpose, while others allow flexibility, and you can use the loan for whatever you want. Ideally, you could get better terms on loans specific to your needs, for example, emergency, medical, or home improvement loans.

Step #5: Prequalification

Some lenders offer prequalification credit checks, soft checks that don't negatively affect your credit score.

Step #6: Loan Rates

You might know the interest rate beforehand, but that doesn't mean you should take the first offer you are given. Compare other lenders' rates and, more importantly, their terms to find a loan offer that doesn't stretch you financially.

Step #7: Loan Application

At this point, you have settled on your ideal lender, so start the application process and submit all the necessary documents.

Step #8: Honor Your Obligation

If the loan is approved, finalize the documents and accept the terms of the contract. You should have the money in your account within 1-2 business days or a week. Submit your payments on time, and make more than the minimum payment whenever possible to reduce your loan burden down the line.

8
TAXES

AKA THE GOVERNMENT'S BEST FRIEND

*"Our new Constitution is now established, everything seems to
promise it will be durable, but, in this
world, nothing is certain except death and taxes."*
—*Benjamin Franklin*

The certainty of taxes highlights its value, not just to our economy but to our very existence. Without taxes, the government wouldn't be able to provide and maintain most, if not all, of the public access facilities we use all the time, like schools, roads, Social Security, recreational parks, police services, and emergency services. Thus, tax is the government's primary source of income, through which it offers these services and makes our lives easier.

Tax is a compulsory contribution paid to the government by every resident in the country. Residents, in this case, are both individuals and companies. In company law, a duly registered company assumes a legal identity similar to a person, such that it can enter into contracts, sue, or be sued in its name. Therefore, once registered or licensed to operate within the country, the company becomes a resident (corporate resident) of the country, also taking up the responsibility of duly paying taxes.

Considering the country's diversity of residents and corporate residents, it would be unfair to have a one-size-fits-all taxation system. This would mean that everyone paid the same tax rate, despite their differences in income and other characteristics. The government's solution to this problem was to create different types and levels of taxation such that the burden of funding the economy is proportionately distributed among residents.

TYPES OF TAXES

One of the reasons why many people run into problems with the IRS is because they aren't aware of their obligation or liability to pay certain taxes. This is usually because they don't understand the different types of taxes. There are various taxes, some of which you probably might not come across your entire life. To make things easier, we'll create three distinct groups you can relate to. These three groups will be your earnings, purchases, and possessions.

Taxes on Earnings

• **Income Tax**

This is a percentage of earned income from the federal or state government at each payment cycle. Interestingly, as of August 2022, the states of Nevada, Florida, Alaska, Wyoming, Texas, Tennessee, and South Dakota did not impose income tax on their residents. This income deficit is, however, recovered by reducing some services or through other classes of taxes, like property tax. Alaska, for example, is one of the most expensive places to live in, despite having the lowest tax book in 2021.

- **Payroll Tax**

For working residents, this is part of your income withheld and remitted by the government by your employer.

Taxes on Purchases

- **Excise Tax**

These taxes are levied on goods, services, or activities and can be imposed on manufacturers, consumers, or retailers. Excise tax can also be charged as *sin tax* to discourage certain activities by making them more expensive. For example, an additional tax on cigarettes is imposed to deter consumption and hopefully reduce the associated healthcare costs or tax on betting.

- **Gross Receipts Tax (GRT)**

This is a tax on the gross sales in your business, regardless of whether you made a profit or loss, and before you account for your expenses. GRT is another unpopular tax, especially for startups, because despite generally making losses in the formative years, you'll still be paying GRT. It's even worse if your business requires a multi-layered production process because GRT is levied at every stage of the production process but is eventually passed down to the final consumer.

- **Sales Tax**

This is a retail tax on goods and services, and you'll see it on most of your receipts. Like property tax, sales tax is another significant contributor to local and state government revenues. Apart from Delaware, Oregon, Alaska, New Hampshire, and Montana, all states in the U.S charge sales tax.

Note that even though consumers are exempt from it, some cities and counties within these states could still levy their own sales tax. Apart from that, you'll also realize that property and income taxes are considerably higher in these states compared to those that charge sales tax to make up for the lost revenue.

- **Value-Added Tax (VAT)**

This tax is usually charged for adding value to a product or service at each stage in its production life cycle. It is the most popular tax imposed on consumables, with the final consumer paying the total VAT. For example, suppose you pay VAT on a book. In that case, you are paying for the value added in converting the logs or recycled material into paper, refining the paper into a reasonable size that suits your needs, and so on.

Taxes on Possessions

- **Estate and Inheritance Tax**

These are taxes on the value of your property at the time of your demise. Inheritance tax is usually paid by beneficiaries to the property, while the estate tax is charged on your estate, and the balance is distributed to your heirs. Due to the complexity of levying these taxes and the fact that, like wealth tax, they can discourage investment, most states stopped charging them.

- **Property Tax**

Property tax is one of the most important sources of income for local and state governments and is charged on immovable property like buildings and land. It's one of the biggest contributors to local government's ability to fund key services like emergency medical services, fire department, police services, roads, and schools.

• Tangible Personal Property (TPP) Tax

This is a tax on property like furniture, machinery, inventory, and equipment used in your business, which can be physically relocated. It is levied annually on the value of your income-earning assets.

• Wealth Tax

Also known as equity or capital tax is the amount of tax charged yearly on the market value of your net wealth exceeding a specific limit. Your net wealth, in this case, represents all your assets after accounting for debts in that year. For example, if your combined assets are worth $100,000 but you owe a total of $30,000, your wealth tax will be levied against $70,000 because that's all you own.

Wealth tax is quite an unpopular tax because it generally targets wealthy persons. Most of these are people who, discouraged by the tax, can quickly move their wealth to countries with friendlier tax policies, especially where wealth tax isn't levied. It's also often seen as a disincentive to investment, discouraging wealthy entrepreneurs from investing in the country.

Failure to pay taxes is a grave disservice to the country because you deny the crucial government revenue it needs to provide vital services to everyone, including yourself and your loved ones. Granted, people are generally hard-pressed when paying taxes, despite their awareness of the importance of taxation to the economy. Left to our own devices, most people would prefer not to pay taxes. This is why governments have agencies like the Internal Revenue Service (IRS) to enforce tax policies and compliance, failure to which you could face hefty fines or jail time.

9

RETIREMENT

PLANNING FOR THE SUNSET YEARS

*W*hat's your idea of retirement?

For most people, retirement means old age, when your productive years are long gone, being frail, and enjoying what remains of your sunset years. I mean, this is the concept of retirement that society has cultured us into for generations.

One of Merriam-Webster's definitions of retirement that we'll dwell on is withdrawal from your occupation, position, or active working life. You don't necessarily have to wait to retire when you are too old to work. Many young people today espouse this concept of retirement and talk of retiring in their 30s or 40s.

Even though many people dream of retiring young, very few get to do it. It's quite an achievement to retire and enjoy the rest of your life while still energetic. This means your retirement isn't limited to life in assisted living facilities and other kinds of support commonly reserved for the elderly. Instead, retirement life for you could mean traveling the world, taking an active role in your children's lives as they grow up, investing more time in your hobbies, and so on. You retire to enjoy life, not what's left of it.

The most important step in retirement planning is today. At this very moment, what are you doing to prepare for retirement? Retirement planning shouldn't start when you've settled into your job because, for most people, that never happens. As soon as you get a job, bills, taxes, contributions to different causes, helping out a friend or family member, loans, mortgages, and so on. Before you know it, you've been working for 20 years, and events have overtaken your idea of retirement planning. Next thing you know, you are barely 10 years away from retirement, and that's when the reality hits you that you don't have much to live on when you retire.

Let's briefly go over some interesting statistics you should keep in mind. Did you know that in 2020, at least 32% of Americans admitted having saved nothing for retirement? (Petrov, 2020).

Imagine that a third of the population would be financially devastated if they were to retire today. Granted, 2020 was a challenging year for everyone, given the Covid pandemic and economic turmoil that ensued. Still, the reality is that these people had no retirement plans before the pandemic year. It gets worse because the pandemic left more people in financial distress than before, despite widespread hope that life would get better beyond 2021.

The tragedy of our life is that most working population plans to keep working even after retirement. How tragic, you might ask. Well, more than 70% of the working population. That's almost everyone you can think of. It's crazy and heart-wrenching to imagine your retirement plan is to keep working, being 70 and still putting in the manual hours, sitting in traffic, pushing reports, and so on.

Despite the alarming statistics, this doesn't have to be your reality. The secret to successful retirement planning is to start right now; even with the little you have, come up with a plan and start working on it.

IMPORTANCE OF RETIREMENT PLANNING

Retirement is a personal choice, so everyone has different needs that inform their need for retirement planning. That being said, here are some vital points to show you the value of retirement planning and why you should start right away:

• **The Value of Compounding**

One of the best things about investing in your retirement from today is that you have more years to benefit from compound interest than someone who starts it later. Compounding means your retirement savings earn interest on interest already earned, thereby growing your account exponentially.

• **Easy Contributions**

Starting your retirement savings early allows you to make small, manageable contributions to the account, which is better than having to make larger catch-up contributions as you get closer to your ideal retirement age. Besides, you'll also capitalize on the compounding value of your investment.

• **Tax Benefits**

Most employee retirement contributions usually attract tax benefits. Common examples include the traditional IRA and

401(k) accounts, where your contributions are tax-free until you withdraw from the account. Other than that, these are also tax-deductible contributions, allowing you to reduce your overall tax burden by lowering your taxable income.

- **The Case for Social Security**

The stability of the government's Social Security benefits program isn't guaranteed, with the trust fund facing possible depletion by around 2034-2035. The government must consider drastic measures like reducing anticipated benefits for retirees.

If the current monthly benefit of around $1,400 is hardly dependable for the usual expenses, imagine the prospect of unreliability in future changes. It would be safer to have another source of retirement income, hence the need for retirement savings.

- **Ultimate Comfort**

You last want to struggle financially in your sunset years, even if you retire young. This is why it makes sense to start saving as early as now. Whatever age you decide to retire, you'd be more comfortable knowing you can relax without worrying about money.

HOW MUCH DO I NEED TO RETIRE COMFORTABLY?

We have to emphasize the word comfortably in this case because there's a huge difference between retiring and retiring comfortably. Retiring could be for various reasons, from illness to old age, so the decision to retire might not be within your control. Retiring comfortably, on the other hand, means being financially prepared and ready for retirement, which in most cases, is usually retiring on your terms.

The definition of a comfortable lifestyle in retirement is different for every person. However, the general consensus is that you need roughly 80% of your annual income. This means that if you earned $60,000 annually before you retired, you'd need at least $48,000 every year to retire comfortably.

This is a rough estimate, as the actual figure will depend on your intentions once you retire. For example, if you plan to travel the world, you'll need more money.

Once you've established how much you'll need when you retire, the next step is how to save that amount. Note that the amount you need for retirement can change throughout your employment life cycle. For example, you could set aside a percentage of your income every month for retirement. If you start saving today, you can put aside 15% of your gross income.

The target amount you need to retire changes comfortably as you grow older. For example, by the time you are 40, your retirement account should have at least three times your annual salary, six times by 50, and eight times by 60. Beyond 60, you should have ten times your annual salary saved for retirement.

There are many other approaches you can use to help you stay focused on the target amount required for retirement. Whichever of these you use, the most important thing is to stay focused and keep contributing to the retirement fund.

PREPARING FOR RETIREMENT

You can't just wake up one day and be fully prepared for retirement. Retirement planning takes time, effort, commitment, and, most importantly, money. Most people crave financial security in retirement but barely put in the work. Here are some valuable ideas that will help you prepare for retirement:

1. Employment Retirement Savings Plan

Make regular contributions to the retirement savings plan available in your place of work, like a 401(k) plan. Your employer's contribution will give you a considerable amount to fall back on when you retire.

If your employer doesn't have a retirement savings plan, talk to them about it, and encourage them to get one going. Several retirement savings plans are available that you can both invest in and benefit from.

Assuming that your employer has a pension plan, find out what it involves and what it covers. Review the individual benefit statement to figure out how much you stand to gain from the pension plan. If you change employment, find out whether you might be due certain benefits from your previous employer.

2. Social Security Benefits

There's a lot of debate around Social Security at the moment, especially the fact that the trust fund is almost depleted, so the government will have to institute new measures in the future to keep the plan going. Find out more about how this might affect your future retirement plans, and start working on a contingency plan.

3. Individual Retirement Account (IRA)

This is a tax-advantaged account that will boost your retirement savings plan. For example, between now and the time you turn 50, you can keep contributing up to $6,000 annually. You have the option of a traditional IRA or the Roth IRA.

4. Goal-Oriented Saving

Start saving, and keep going if you have been doing it already. Make saving a habit, and remember that you are saving for a purpose. On the same note, try to avoid withdrawing from your retirement savings. In most cases, you'll incur withdrawal penalties and lose both the principal and interest earned.

5. Learn About Investment

This is also a good opportunity to explore other valuable lessons about investing. Learn about dividends, diversification, inflation, and anything else that might affect your investment. The right investment mix, especially for a diversified portfolio, will change over time in response to changing economic conditions.

6. Needs Assessment

Don't just save blindly. When you retire, figure out what you intend to do, and save with that in mind. This will also help you determine whether your target amount will be sufficient.

Even though the points above will generally set you on the right path to retirement planning, things keep changing in the world of finance, so you'll need new information from time to time. Don't be afraid to ask the difficult questions, whether to your employer, bank, financial advisor, or anyone else who might be in a position to assist. You'd instead ask the questions and get answers because your future is at stake.

THE GOVERNMENT'S SUPPORT ONCE YOU RETIRE

Contrary to what most people believe, Medicare and Social Security aren't the only government-backed programs for retirees. Many other programs are available, but for different reasons, many people don't participate in them. Common reasons for this include the complexity of the application process and the fact that most people don't know about some of these programs.

To make your work easier, we'll discuss the programs in three broad categories so that you can plan along the programs depending on your future retirement needs.

Healthcare Support Programs

Despite its popularity, medicare isn't the only healthcare program for retired citizens. Every state, for example, runs a Medicare Savings Program, which should cater to your copayments, coinsurance, deductibles, and Medicare premiums. The savings programs have different benefits and limits so you can find out more from the Medicaid program office in your state.

- **Medicaid**

This state and federal government-sponsored program are for persons with limited resources or income that pays for some healthcare needs, such as drugs, transportation, x-rays, hospital services, home health services, and visits to healthcare service providers.

- **VA Health Care Programs**

These programs are for military veterans. Other than affiliation to the military service, benefits upon qualification generally depend on the military unit you served and your age.

Housing Support Programs

Your housing arrangements might change for different reasons once you retire. You might have to make some repairs or modifications for more effortless mobility. Retirement might sometimes mean moving to nursing homes or assisted living facilities. Here are some government-sponsored programs that could be useful:

• **Housing Counseling**

You can get HUD-sponsored counseling services through approved agents on issues like credit challenges, foreclosures, bankruptcies, and defaults, which many people struggle with once they retire.

• **Low Income Home Energy Assistance Program (LIHEAP)**

This is a cash grant program for affordable heating and cooling bills. Note that despite retirees and persons living with disabilities being the target for this program, there was no age limit for qualification at the time of this publication. Qualification is only based on your income, which varies in every state.

• **Home Equity Conversion Mortgages (HECMs)**

This is a unique reverse mortgage program under the Federal Housing Administration (FHA), specifically for older homeowners. Through this program, you can withdraw part of your home's equity (ownership) as a loan.

• Housing Choice Voucher

This is a U.S. Department of Housing and Urban Development (HUD) program that allows low-income retirees from 62 years old housing support. Unfortunately, this program has a notoriously long waiting list, so it's best to consider other alternatives while you wait.

• Section 504 Housing Repair Program

Also known as the USDA Housing Repair Program, this provides low-interest loans and grants toward home improvements and repairs for low-income earning retirees.

• Private Rent Subsidies

This subsidy program targets landlords housing low-income seniors in rental homes, including private houses and apartments.

Income Support Programs

You probably won't be receiving income from what used to be your primary source of income, primarily if you were formally employed. Other than a passive source of income, if you created one, you might not have much to work with. Here are some government-backed programs you can consider:

• Social Security

You make contributions to the government's trust fund throughout your working life, and they send you a monthly stipend once you retire for the rest of your life.

• Supplemental Security Income (SSI)

This program provides financial aid to blind or disabled, low-income citizens at least 65 years of age. The expected benefits depend on your living situation, income, and continued eligibility.

- **Senior Community Service Employment Program (SCSEP)**

This Department of Labor initiative encourages senior citizens to pursue long-term employment from paid community services and learn new skills like computer programming.

- **Federal Employee Retirement System (FERS)**

This program is strictly for federal government retirees, allowing you a consistent monthly annuity payment once you retire.

- **Retirement Savings Plans**

The government, through the IRS, supports retirement savings plans like the IRAs and 401(k) by allowing you some tax benefits on your contributions.

Nutrition Support Programs

Through different state programs, the federal government offers nutritional support to low-income retirees, seniors, and other individuals who qualify throughout the country. Here are some of the programs you can consider:

- **Child and Adult Care Food Program (CACFP)**

This USDA-sponsored program provides nutritious snacks and meals to eligible seniors in adult daycare programs.

- **The Emergency Food Assistance Program (TEFAP)**

This is a USDA-sponsored program that distributes food to low-income senior citizens through soup kitchens and food banks in every state.

- **Senior Farmers' Market Nutrition Program (SFMNP)**

In this program, qualified low-income senior citizens receive coupon booklets to pay for produce at the local farmers' markets. Note that the coupons can only be used for perishable foods. However, some farmers' markets don't accept coupons, so it's always wise to confirm where they are applicable.

- **Supplemental Nutrition Assistance Program (SNAP)**

You might probably know them as food stamps. This program offers stipends to eligible low-income seniors, which they can use to buy food. Since these are state-run programs, the stipend amount varies in every state and depends on your income level.

- **Commodity Supplemental Food Program (CSFP)**

Instead of meals, as provided through the CACFP, this USDA program provides food to eligible low-income senior citizens.

Tax Assistance Programs

Your tax obligation changes after retirement, and your tax liability are mostly weighed against the amount you earn from different sources of income and whether you use the tax deductions available to you. Here are some programs that might interest you:

- **Tax Counseling for the Elderly (TCE)**

This is an IRS-sponsored program that provides free tax consulting services to the elderly.

- **Tax Credit for Older People and Those with Disabilities**

If you fit the profile outlined in IRS Publication 524, you can get some tax credits as long as your income falls within the eligibility criteria.

• **Volunteer Income Tax Assistance (VITA)**

If your annual income doesn't exceed $58,000, you might qualify for this program, especially if you are disabled or struggle with English.

As you can see from the options above, various government-sponsored programs could come in handy once you retire, especially in your sunset years. This information might also be useful if you live with or are taking care of a senior citizen because applying for some of these programs could significantly reduce your financial burden.

* * *

10

MULTIPLE INCOME STREAMS

WHEN PAYCHECKS JUST AREN'T ENOUGH

*"If you don't have big dreams and goals, you'll
end up working for someone that does."*
—Unknown

G rowing up, my parents stressed the importance of having my own business. They had theirs going, so to them, it was only natural that I followed in their footsteps. However, they probably didn't know, but I was not too fond of that idea.

In my experience with my parents, owning a business meant toiling away during school breaks, rolling egg rolls, and answering phone calls, while my friends enjoyed their school breaks meeting Mickey Mouse and doing all kinds of fun things. There was no way I was going to sign up for that idea.

Even worse, my parents were too busy (understandably), so my brother and I were alone at our elementary and middle school graduations. He was 11 months younger, but we were in the same grade. One of my friends' parents was kind enough to drive me to these important milestones in my life.

During those years, it never occurred to me why my parents opted for this career path with constant exhaustion at the end of the day, every day. Perhaps I was too young to understand it back then, but owning a business meant there wasn't a limit to how much my parents could earn. Imagine that, unlimited earnings potential! Well, in retrospect, I know so much better today.

As I grew up, it dawned on me that besides the unlimited earnings potential, owning a business also meant that I had one thing that most people don't, a job. Picture that, every day, you'd wake up to the reassuring sense of having a job. This is in a society where people wake up to job cuts, companies downsizing, and so on. Heck! Neither of my parents had the luxury or liberty of a job when they came to America.

Side hustles, passive incomes, whatever name you want to assign them, are crucial in realizing your financial goals. The beauty of a side hustle is that other than putting in extra work, the income potential is excellent. If you're already working, there's so much you could do with an additional source of income in this economy. If you mortgage a house, you could clear the loan years ahead of schedule, freeing up your money for other things.

Passive income? Well, if you're like most people, one paycheck might never be enough to meet all your needs. Passive income means having your money work for you, so much that you make money while you sleep. Wouldn't that be amazing? Side hustles are the simplest gateway to passive income. Passive income, on the other hand, is your gateway out of the rat race, out of living from paycheck to paycheck.

LIVING PAYCHECK TO PAYCHECK

According to a report published by CBS in 2019, advocacy group Prosperity Now found that more than 40% of Americans were on the brink of poverty. Interestingly, when we talk about poverty, many people think about the homeless or other people who are already down on their luck. Unfortunately, the true picture of poverty captures so many, including those who are actively employed. In particular, the highlight of the report was that the surveyed individuals were people who had jobs but ran the risk of their lives turning for the worst with a single missed paycheck.

This was a 2019 report. Since then, we've had the global economy ravaged by COVID, followed by rising inflation and the impact of the Russia-Ukraine conflict. You'd imagine the statistics, should a similar study be conducted today, would paint quite a grim picture. We could speculate that perhaps more than 50% of the population would be on the brink.

The reality of this report was that most people couldn't sustain their current standard of living if their incomes were to be abruptly disrupted. This is what we call liquid-asset poor. You don't have enough money set aside for emergencies.

If things ever go south, millions of people would struggle to afford a decent meal or housing. It is terrifying to imagine that at least four in every ten people you meet could already have their fate so sealed. It's so sad that savings accounts or an emergency stash are unheard of in most households. In difficult moments, such households are left at the mercy of whatever might befall them.

If your life is held together by the promptness of your paychecks, you honestly are one late paycheck away from being homeless. Merriam-Webster defines living paycheck to paycheck as spending all your money from the previous paycheck before you receive the next one. This basically means you are always at a deficit. Your money disappears as soon as it comes in, and then you have to wait for the next paycheck, and life goes on.

How bad can things get?

In this situation, most people can't afford to see a doctor when they are sick. They'd instead seek over-the-counter medication or stay at home and ride out the illness. This also means less income because they won't be paid for days away from work, further straining an already struggling household.

In summary, living paycheck to paycheck means you'll soon be unable to afford food, housing, and good health. Not such a good place to be, right?

* * *

ESCAPING THE RAT RACE

You've probably heard the phrase a few times already, but have you ever stopped to wonder what exactly is the "rat race"? How do you know you are in it? How do you get out of it?

I can tell you one thing about the rat race—it is a life of unending exhaustion. It drains you financially, emotionally, mentally, and in every sense of your being. The rat race is an unpleasant daily work routine that involves working extremely hard to compete for status, power, money, and other trappings of the employment lifestyle. It never ends. It's an unfair tradeoff between your time and the money you receive throughout your working life.

The worst thing about being trapped in the rat race is that nothing good really comes out of it for you. All your hard work, time, and effort go to serving the needs of investors and business owners. From time to time, you'll get some financial rewards, bonuses, and trips. You name it. But none of that will ever compare to what the executives get, or at the very least, the effort you put in throughout the year. It's no wonder some people call it corporate servitude.

Why does everyone want to escape the rat race? The simple answer: To save your life. There's so much more to life than slaving your productive years away in some corporate machine. You need to live a quality life, spend more time with your loved ones, go on trips, and do things you enjoy. Despite the periodic financial perks, life in the rat race can only promise you bills, taxes, and eventually death.

Let's discuss tips on how to escape or avoid the rat race and introduce some quality into your life because, let's face it, you deserve a good life.

• Living Paycheck to Paycheck

Even though we discussed this in the previous section, being in this situation is a valid reason to want to turn your life around. Not having sufficient money to meet your needs isn't a good place financially, especially for someone who earns an income.

• The Tipping Point

Why exactly are you so bummed about being in the rat race? What is it about this life that has pushed your limits? In life, all outstanding achievements start with having a purpose. It gives you a sense of direction and fuels your commitment to the cause.

Perhaps you are tired of the backstabbing and other toxic traits of corporate life, or you can't stand another minute working for your boss—the burning fire in you, the rage and frustration, channels that into overcoming your misery.

• Rethink Your Priorities

The first thing that comes to mind as soon as you get your paycheck is to clear debts, pay bills, and so on. Before you know it, you have nothing left but to look forward to the next paycheck. Switch things up a bit, and make yourself a priority.

Set a fixed amount you pay yourself monthly for all the hard work. It could be $50 or $100, whatever you feel is right, and take it off the paycheck before you address the other financial commitments. If your money doesn't add up at the end of it all, then it's time for you to start thinking of an additional source of income.On the same note, stop spending on things you don't need. In fact, cut up that credit card. Spend on essentials, and try to live within your means as much as possible. If you can save some money, put it into a long-term investment plan.

• Asset Acquisition

We mentioned earlier that most people are liquid-asset poor. Therefore, it's only fitting that you try to own some assets, especially those that can earn you some income. Buy some stocks, bonds, or trade options, some rental property, sign up as an Uber driver, and so on. The point here is to own assets that can be a reliable source of income.

On the same note, your greatest and most profitable asset is yourself. What can you do to derive more value from yourself? You could invest in a side hustle. We only mentioned rideshare above, but there are so many options you can think of. Apart from that, you can also invest in yourself by learning new skills, for example, marketing and sales. This will help you promote and grow your side hustle.

• Savings and Investments

One of the reasons why you might be in the rat race is because you don't have any savings or investments to your name. Naturally, you must fix that. Start saving today. It might be a small amount, but collectively, it will be worth so much in the long run. A savings culture goes hand in hand with investment. Investment is letting your money work for you—stocks, real estate, cryptocurrency, you name it. Research it well and understand the risks involved in every investment opportunity before committing your money.

• The Need for Outsourcing

Once your side hustle is set up, you should think about outsourcing. Ideally, this means getting the best talent to help you grow the business, usually at a fraction of the cost. For example, get a social media expert to grow your presence online and a search engine optimization pro to boost your visibility and rankings on Google. Other than working with professionals, outsourcing helps you avoid overworking.

• Time to Walk Away

There comes a time when you simply shut down and walk away from the rat race. For some people, that day comes as a surprise. For others, it's all part of an elaborate plan. Freedom! That last time you sign out of the office and walk away from the rat race, never looking back. It's a new experience: not waking up early to beat the morning rush; no longer having to sit in traffic. It might be unsettling for a while, but as soon as you get out of the rat race, you start working hard not to get sucked back in.

Ultimately, the trappings of the rat race, usually in the form of job security, regular paychecks, and so on, are no more than a facade. It's not until a global crisis like the COVID pandemic that many people realize how expendable they are, and the notion of job security is a fallacy. Besides, with technological advancements, companies will continue to work towards automation to reduce their expenditure on salaries and other employee-related costs. Thus, no one is ever truly secure in their jobs. Start working on an exit strategy today because true independence is something no employer will ever give you. But, once you find and embrace it, you'll never want to give it up.

Now that we've covered the rat race at length, here's something you need to think about: What's your next move once you realize that your paycheck barely covers your monthly expenses?

MULTIPLE SOURCES OF INCOME

If you're here, there's a good chance you already understand that your paycheck alone won't cut it. You need more money coming in every month to meet your needs and live a comfortable, happy life. This is why multiple income streams are essential. With different sources of income, usually coming in at different times of the month, you will never be in the wrong position if any of them delay or don't come at all.

Why is it Necessary?

The beauty of life today is that the digital ecosystem has matured so much over the years that you have access to lots of opportunities to make more money beyond your primary paycheck. Let's briefly discuss some reasons why you need multiple sources of income:

● **More Money**

Let's face it, who doesn't want more money? If the wealthy already have more money than they'll ever need for generations to come and are always looking for ways of earning more, why shouldn't they?

Having more money gives you more freedom and access to opportunities for investment and growth that you wouldn't have before. You can clear debts faster, enroll in professional courses, and learn in-demand skills. However, while having more money is a good thing, you must be careful not to fall into the lifestyle inflation trap.

● **Early Retirement**

Having multiple sources of income means you can check things off your bucket list earlier in life. If you meet all or most of your life goals early, you honestly don't have to work to retire in your 60s. Today many people are retiring in their 30s and 40s simply because they've attained their life goals and can focus on whatever brings them happiness. You could even travel the world if you wanted.

● **Financial Security**

If you are working a 9-5, I can guarantee you that you have no control over your fate. Layoffs are part of corporate life, and your position might be deemed redundant at any time.

Even executives are let go all the time, so clearly, anyone is replaceable.

Multiple income streams give you true financial security because you'll always be in charge. Besides, even if your employer lets you go, you'll still have some money coming in, so you won't fall into poverty. If anything, you'll be able to commit more time to grow your side hustles and earn even more money.

WHO WANTS TO BE A MILLIONAIRE?

Of course, you want more commas in your bank account before the decimal point. You probably won't make millions overnight, but every additional source of income you create gets you one step closer to your first million, and then the next, and so on. It takes a bit of work, okay, a lot of work, but the incremental value of your input means that you are in a better financial position every month than the previous month.

Multiple income sources also mean your network is expanding exponentially. This is where you'll strike strategic partnerships, deals, and so on that help you get that financial breakthrough.

THE POWER OF DIVERSITY

Think about humanity for a moment. Our diversity is one of the reasons for the great inventions and successes we've had over the years. Our strengths supplement other people's weaknesses, as theirs do your shortcomings. No one can be good at everything, so why should you expect the same of your money?

A single source of income will never be good enough for all your needs. Multiple sources, however, can. This allows you to spread your money around, reducing the strain on your paycheck. If you do it right, you probably won't even need that paycheck anymore. If anything, some people hardly touch their paychecks. That money automatically goes to a savings or investment account because their other income sources meet all their needs.

So, in a bid to diversify your sources of income, here are some examples you can think about:

1. Smart investments like the Roth IRA, stock market, bonds, and options trading
2. Rental income, which also has some good tax benefits
3. Work hard to get more employee benefits if you wish to stay employed
4. Tap into the gig economy with partners like Airbnb, Uber, and Lyft
5. Start an online business

Given all the information we've discussed herein, at this point, the only thing standing between you and escaping the rat race is your imagination.

SIDE HUSTLES

Having a side hustle is the in-thing today, so much that it seems everyone has one. A side hustle is any employment you engage in other than your full-time job. People mostly start side hustles to supplement their primary income, but over the years, it's become apparent that side hustles have more potential. Your side hustle can be so successful that you quit your full-time job, focus on it, and even create employment opportunities for others.

In the beginning, the concept of a side hustle is that you work on it outside your day job hours. This is why most people work on them during the evenings, weekends, and holidays. Since you're working in your free time, most side hustles are on a part-time basis, contracts, freelance, or you could be available on call. One of the best things about a side hustle is that, other than the additional income, it helps you smoothen the transition to quitting your full-time job.

Personally, I never understood why or how my age-mates couldn't hold down a side hustle. Aside from my full-time job managing my parents' very busy store, I also publish books and do catering for parties from time to time. And keep in mind that I work roughly 60 hours a week at my parent's store, and even then, I'm STILL trying to find new side hustles to expand my bank account.

The Benefits

Why should you set up a side hustle? Here are some of the benefits you can look forward to:

• **Ultimate Satisfaction**

Side hustles are an opportunity to pursue and monetize your hobbies and passions. You could also use it as a stepping stone to your dream job. So, in the long run, a side hustle can help you find purpose in your life, away from the trappings of formal employment.

• **Financial Freedom**

The extra money could be useful in clearing debts, investing, or creating an emergency savings fund, all of which will be useful in the future. It gives you more flexibility in financial decision-making, so you don't have to strain your budget constantly.

• **Flexibility**

Unlike demanding office hours, you are primarily in charge of your side hustle, so you get to decide when and how long you can work. For someone tired of the inflexibility of a 9-5, this can be a welcome change that uplifts your spirits.

Besides, you are not mandated to clock in a certain amount of time in the side hustle. You can work on it as your time and energy allow.

• **Ease of Entry**

Most side hustles don't require large amounts of funds to set up, mainly when you offer services. You might also not need an expensive degree to get going. It's all about using your skills to create value in customers' lives.

Potential Pitfalls

Don't let the allure of more income fool you. Side hustles require a lot of effort to build and grow. Similarly, there will be some challenges along the way. Remember that to pluck some roses, you must always contend with the thorns. Here are some potential challenges you might experience in your side hustle:

• **Exhaustion**

Imagine going through a busy work week and returning home to work on your side hustle in the evenings and weekends. This should be your relaxation and unwinding time. Instead, you are trying to make more money. Devoting time to your side hustle can potentially strain your relationships because you'll barely have time for yourself, let alone other people in your life.

• The Rate Card Problem

Left to their own devices, many people struggle to set the correct value for their work. It's always a thin line between overpricing or underpricing your work in side hustles. This is mostly because there are no set industry guidelines, as is the case in the corporate sector. Instead, most engagements involve negotiations with your customers.

• Ownership Stress

This is your pet project, so you must devote more than your time for it to succeed. You'll mostly be in charge of everything from filing taxes to record-keeping and marketing your business. Even though you can outsource most of these services, you'll still have to make the final call on quality assurances, often pushing you out of your comfort zone and making your life more stressful.

• The Unwelcome Distractions

As your side hustle grows, expect it to consume more time and attention, primarily because you are going for nothing short of success. Unfortunately, the ensuing pursuit might distract you from your day job, which, as your primary source of income, could affect your deliverables, creating problems with your supervisors and superiors. You could lose that job before you are ready to quit it.

For context, here are some side hustles you can start without a substantial financial investment:

1. become a virtual assistant or any type of freelancer
2. coach a sport you love
3. advertise for brands on your car
4. food, grocery, and alcohol delivery services
5. offer tutoring services
6. party catering
7. rent your car or rideshare
8. pet sitting, house sitting, babysitting, or even virtual sitting
9. landscaping services
10. become a tour guide for your city
11. sell your items on online marketplaces
12. offer cleaning services of any kind

As you can see above, there's so much you can do in your spare time to earn extra income. Don't restrict yourself to this list, though, because it barely scratches the surface of the kind of side hustle opportunities available.

Side hustles are great, but not everyone has the time or desire to work extra hours after a long day in the office. If this describes you, but you have some money set aside, you can think of passive income.

To quote award-winning author and businessman Robert Kiyosaki, "don't work for money; make it work for you."

* * *

PASSIVE INCOME

Passive income represents any source of income that doesn't require your direct or active involvement. In a broad sense, this is what people mean when they say to make money while you sleep. Side hustles can help you earn passive income, especially once the business grows and becomes autonomous. For example, if you set up an online gaming platform, you will be actively involved in the beginning. This is active income. However, once the platform grows and gamers sign in, pay, and play regularly, you only put in minimal effort to get paid. This is the point where it becomes a passive source of income. The business earns you income even without your physical presence.

Passive Income Pros

What's so important about passive income that you should consider it?

• Multiplicity of Time

We all have 24 hours in a day, most of which your employer owns. Passive income allows you to expand your horizons, tapping into more hours than you physically have. For example, if you have three sources of passive income, that's the equivalent of having three extra income days within your 24-hour day without missing a day of your regular job. It would be safe to say you have 96 hours in a day!

Speaking of time, having multiple sources of passive income means you don't have to commit your free time to look for more money anymore. You can spend it with your loved ones, relax and have a good time without worrying about money.

• Financial Stability and Freedom

The fact that you no longer depend on your primary paycheck for everything makes you more confident about your life, such that you aren't concerned by things like job cuts, injury, or illness. This is particularly important when you have a family.

Most sources of passive income can be managed remotely. It could be anything from an online business to a diversified investment portfolio, including shares and stock options. You can live anywhere in the world.

Ultimately, this stability and flexibility culminate into financial independence. It feels good knowing you have all the money you need to cater to your family's needs without having to work actively. At this point, nothing can stop you from retiring early.

• Debt-free Life

Once your passive income streams start paying off, one of the first things you should do is pay off your debts to ease the burden off your paycheck. You can easily pay off your debts sooner, for example, in three years instead of five years, reducing the amount of money you might have lost in the transaction costs.

• Tax Considerations

Wherever money, especially income, is involved, taxes are never too far behind. Once you set up your passive income streams, it's good to learn about their tax implications to understand where you might qualify for tax breaks. Speak to a tax attorney to advise you accordingly.

Passive Income Cons

Like running a side hustle, you might encounter some challenges during your passive income ventures. Let's look at some of them to help prepare you for what lies ahead:

• How to Get Started

This will mostly depend on the sort of business you intend to set up. Some businesses require a large initial investment, so you might need to dig deeper into your pockets for this. This might also leave you exposed financially if the business fails.

• The Curse of Success

Success is awesome. You can finally afford to buy your desired things without asking for a loan. You might even quit your day job. However, the other unfortunate reality of success is that it can get quite lonely. It might not be possible to interact with your friends and family as often as you used to.

• Spreading Yourself Too Thin

Some people have done it, but depending on the kind of income stream you set up, it might be practically impossible to quit your day job and cover all your expenses and emergencies on a single source of passive income. To generate that kind of money every month, you'd have to set up multiple sources of income.

• There's Nothing Passive About It

When you talk about passive income, people generally assume you've set up an autonomous system that earns you income without lifting a finger. This isn't true. It takes a lot of effort, time, and other resources to set up a thriving source of passive income, not forgetting the maintenance and management costs where applicable.

Ultimately, it's always wise to consider the pros and cons of any opportunity and weigh them against your personal goals and objectives to see if it aligns with your vision for the future. Here are some passive income ideas that you can put through the magnifying glass and use as your ticket to financial freedom:

1. become a social media influencer
2. sell digital products online
3. blogging
4. offer online translation services
5. stream video games online
6. create YouTube content
7. write and sell ebooks
8. offer rental storage services
9. invest in real estate
10. invest in stocks

Speaking of investments, you must exercise due diligence at all times, as our society is rife with scammers and other criminals looking to exploit you whenever an opportunity arises. For example, one of my close associates lost around $50,000, not in the stock market but trying to invest in the stock market.

It's quite a common scam. He met someone who was going to 'teach' him how to invest in stocks and time the market. This, unfortunately, was a scam that many people fall into. It got worse because this victim believed that the 'teacher' would have been more willing to assist if they received more money, despite wiring close to $50,000.

Scammers generally try to recruit more people into the scam, so once they lure you in, they'll try to tap into your close associates through you. Before you know it, you've recruited your family and close friends into the trap. As a rule of thumb, never invest your money in something you don't know or don't fully understand. This is a mantra Warren Buffet lives by.

* * *

CONCLUSION

I've learned so much about life and finance over the years. However, one of the most humbling lessons was that many of my peers had no clue about personal finances. I saw this in high school, college, and, unfortunately, even in my professional life. It is a worrying trend, especially when you consider the fact that the global economy has been hurting for a while.

Challenging economic times demand that we make difficult decisions at a personal level. Unfortunately, most people don't know how to do that. The high cost of living and rising inflation mean that your money will usually hardly afford you the same things it has achieved. For many people, borrowing money is the only way to plug this deficit. If you are already in debt, such a situation can quickly plunge you deeper into debt.

The information discussed in this book will help you make smarter financial decisions. You are in a better position today because you are getting this information early. Most people start thinking about financial literacy when things get out of hand, and their finances are messy. Some never learn about money and simply breeze through life with a trial-and-error approach to finances. You are smarter than that.

Financial management isn't just about keeping your finances in order. You learn many lessons along the way, like the importance of delayed gratification, budgeting, and prioritization. These are valuable skills whose value transcends financial management. You learn how to be patient, research information before you buy anything, and, most importantly, have self-discipline.

Financial management is incomplete without self-discipline. You see, money gives you a taste of freedom. When you don't have money, you can't get anything. Once you have money, you are free to buy whatever you want. This freedom, once abused, becomes a one-way ticket to financial ruin. Financial self-discipline is crucial because you realize that not all purchases are as pressing as you think. More often, the urgency preceding a purchase is but a fallacy. Once you wait it out and focus on something else, you soon realize that it isn't as urgent as you imagined. If anything, you probably didn't even need to spend in the first place.

Discipline is also an important virtue in a key pillar of your journey to financial freedom—investment. I've attended many webinars, seminars, meetings, and talks about personal finance and investment, discussing various dynamics of money and investment. The undertone in most of these engagements is usually that the earlier you start investing, the better chances you'll have for prosperity.

You see, no one can predict the future. When you start investing at an early age, you have a lot of room for learning and growth. You will make mistakes; everyone does. But you will learn from them. Think about it for a moment. Would you rather lose $2,000 in a silly investment mistake today or lose $20,000 in the same mistake 15 years from now?

Beginners generally don't spend so much money in investment transactions, either from caution or limited capital. When you start investing today, you will learn, win, and lose. However, the lessons make you bolder and more confident going forward. By the time your portfolio grows to the point where you can commit tens or hundreds of thousands in investments, you'll be wiser and sharper than your peers who are just getting started in the world of investments. This advantage is priceless.

The resounding theme throughout this book is the need to save. Start saving money right away. It might not seem like much at the beginning, but the cumulative impact in the future will be incredible. Besides, creating a saving culture is one of the smartest things you can do with your money. The goal is to reach a point where saving money is second nature to you.

While saving is awesome, it's impossible to save what you don't have. People have different circumstances in life. If you can save some money from your present earnings, get right on it. If you can't, you can save by reviewing your expenses and cutting down where possible. Ultimately, the best way to save money is to create multiple sources of income. This is where the side hustles, hobbies, and passion projects come in.

The good news is that you live in a society that's more receptive to disruptive ideas than ever before. Coupled with widespread internet access, you have the entire world at your fingertips. Let no geographical boundaries limit your imagination. Think hard, think deep, and think outside the box. Learn from someone's idea. Challenge yourself to do the extraordinary. You are living in a generation that's pushing the boundaries of space exploration. Why should you settle for less?

★★★★★

For those of you who stuck with me until the very end,
THANK YOU, THANK YOU, THANK YOU!
(You are my new favorite person!)

If you've enjoyed this book, please leave a review.

Your reviews not only help readers choose their next book
but also help me get the word out about financial literacy.

Your reviews can be short and straight to the point; they
don't need to be lengthy.

★★★★★

Kindly use the link or QR code below to leave a review.
https://www.amazon.com/review/create-review/?ie=
UTF8&channel=glance-detail&asin=B0BGCG78VS

Wishing you the best in your financial future,
Dakota A. McQueen
★★★★★

REFERENCES

American Home Shield. (2016). *5 Tips to Help Build an Emergency Budget.* Ahs.com; American Home Shield. https://www.ahs.com/home-matters/cost-savers/do-you-have-a-budget-for-emergency/

Araujo, M. (2020, May 3). *How Insurance Works.* The Balance. https://www.thebalance.com/basics-to-help-you-understand-how-insurance-works-4783595

Bajaj | Allianz. (2021, March 31). *Why Do We Need Insurance? Top 5 Reasons Explained | Bajaj Allianz.* Bajaj Allianz. https://www.bajajallianz.-com/blog/knowledgebytes/why-do-we-need-insurance.html

Beers, B. (2021, June 14). *Internet Banks: Pros and Cons.* Investopedia. https://www.investopedia.com/articles/pf/11/benefits-and-drawbacks-of-internet-banks.asp

Bergeron, K. (2016, June 2). *10 Basic Principles of Financial Management.* Quicken; Quicken, Inc. https://www.quicken.com/10-basic-principles-financial-management

Better Money Habits | Bank of America. (2022). *How to Create a Budget in 6 Simple Steps.* Better Money Habits. https://bettermoneyhabits.banko-famerica.com/en/saving-budgeting/creating-a-budget

Bochichio, D. (2021). *Clean Cut Finance.* Cleancutfinance.com. https://clean-cutfinance.com/live-below-your-means/#:~:text=What%20-does%20it%20mean%20to,helps%20you%20reach%20financial%20independence

Brooke, K. (2015, October 7). *Learn their shopping secrets! Kalyn Brooke.* https://kalynbrooke.com/your-money/things-smart-shoppers-do/#:~:text=Smart%20Shoppers%20Know%20their%20Prices,real-ly%20is%20a%20great%20deal

Burnette, M. (2022, July 12). *Compound Interest Calculator - NerdWallet.* NerdWallet. https://www.nerdwallet.com/banking/calcula-tor/compound-interest-calculator#:~:text=Compound%20interest%20al-lows%20your%20savings,period%2C%20typically%20daily%20or%20monthly.

Cain, S. (2021, August 11). *10 Common Financial Mistakes.* Prosper Blog. https://www.prosper.com/blog/10-common-financial-mistakes/

CalculatorSoup, L. (2022). *Simple Interest Calculator A = P(1 + rt).* CalculatorSoup. https://www.calculatorsoup.com/calculators/finan-cial/simple-interest-plus-principal-calculator.php

Calonia, J. (2022, June 9). *How to get a personal loan in 8 steps.* Bankrate; Bankrate.com. https://www.bankrate.com/loans/personal-loans/how-to-get-personal-loan/

REFERENCES

Cambridge Credit Counseling Corp. (2013). *How to Avoid Making Financial Mistakes | Cambridge Credit.* Cambridge-Credit.org. https://www.cambridge-credit.org/how-to-avoid-making-financial-mistakes.html

Capital One. (2021, March 18). *7 Tips on How to Use a Credit Card Responsibly | Capital One.* Capital One. https://www.capitalone.com/learn-grow/money-management/tips-using-credit-responsibly/

Central Bank. (2022). *10 Strategies to Avoid Getting into Debt.* Centralbank.net. https://www.centralbank.net/learning-center/strategies-to-avoid-debt/

Chen, J. (2022, January 13). *Debt.* Investopedia. https://www.investopedia.com/terms/d/debt.asp

College Data. (2021). *How Much Does College Cost? | CollegeData.* CollegeData. https://www.collegedata.com/resources/pay-your-way/whats-the-price-tag-for-a-college-education

College Raptor Staff. (2021, November 9). *Attending a State University: Pros and Cons - College Raptor Blog.* College Raptor Blog. https://www.collegeraptor.com/find-colleges/articles/college-search/pros-cons-attending-state-colleges/

Common Trust FCU. (2019, April 9). *5 Reasons Why Financial Literacy Should be Taught from a Young Age - Common Trust FCU.* Common Trust FCU. https://www.commontrustfcu.org/5-reasons-why-financial-literacy-should-be-taught-from-a-young-age/

Consumer Financial Protection Bureau. (2020, September 1). *What is a credit score? | Consumer Financial Protection Bureau.* Consumer Financial Protection Bureau. https://www.consumerfinance.gov/ask-cfpb/what-is-a-credit-score-en-315/

Credit Law Center. (2017, August 22). *Top 10 Causes of Debt - Credit Law Center.* Credit Law Center | Attorney Based Credit Repair. https://www.creditlawcenter.com/debt/top-10-causes-of-debt/

CreditRepair.com. (2021, April 15). *Needs vs. wants: a guide to understanding your budget.* CreditRepair.com. https://www.creditrepair.com/blog/finance/needs-vs-wants/

Cussen, M. P. (2022, July 13). *Credit Cards vs. Debit Cards: What's the Difference?* Investopedia. https://www.investopedia.com/articles/personal-finance/050214/credit-vs-debit-cards-which-better.asp

Daly, L. (2019, April 8). *The 5 Principles of Personal Finance Everyone Must Follow.* The Motley Fool; The Ascent by The Motley Fool. https://www.fool.com/the-ascent/banks/articles/the-5-principles-of-personal-finance-everyone-must-follow/

DeMarco, J. (2022, June 28). *10 different types of credit cards.* Bankrate; Bankrate.com. https://www.bankrate.com/finance/credit-cards/different-types-of-credit-cards/

DeNicola, L. (2020, June 3). *How to Use a Credit Card to Build Credit.*

REFERENCES

Experian.com; Experian. https://www.experian.com/blogs/ask-experian/how-to-use-a-credit-card-to-build-credit/

DeNicola, L. (2021, February 11). *What Is a Good Credit Score?* Experian.com; Experian. https://www.experian.com/blogs/ask-experian/credit-education/score-basics/what-is-a-good-credit-score/

Detweiler, G. (2020, September 16). *10 Ways to Build Credit Without a Credit Card | Credit.com*. Credit.com. https://www.credit.com/blog/build-credit-without-a-credit-card/

Devaney, T. (2017, September 19). *Hard credit inquiry vs. soft credit inquiry: What they are and why they matter*. Credit Karma. https://www.creditkarma.com/advice/i/hard-credit-inquiries-and-soft-credit-inquiries

EAT Money. (2019, September 11). *7 Types of Personal Budgets — EAT Money*. EAT Money. https://eat.money/7-types-of-personal-budgets/

Education Planner. (2022). *10 Ways to Reduce College Costs*. Educationplanner.org. http://www.educationplanner.org/students/paying-for-school/ways-to-pay/reduce-college-costs.shtml

Edward Jones. (2019). *11 common financial mistakes and how to avoid them*. Edward Jones; https://www.edwardjones.com/us-en/market-news-insights/guidance-perspective/financial-mistakes

Employee Benefits Security Administration. (2019). *TOP 10 WAYS TO PREPARE FOR RETIREMENT*. https://www.dol.gov/sites/dol-gov/files/ebsa/about-ebsa/our-activities/resource-center/publications/top-10-ways-to-prepare-for-retirement.pdf

Epstein, L. (2021, June 20). *Credit Unions vs. Banks: 9 Ways to Decide Which Is Best for You*. Investopedia. https://www.investopedia.com/credit-unions-vs-banks-4590218#:~:text=Credit%20unions%20tend%20to%20have,more%20branches%20and%20ATMs%20nationwide

Ferreira, N. M. (2020, November 9). *How To Escape the Rat Race (And Never Get Sucked Back In)*. Oberlo.com. https://www.oberlo.com/blog/escape-the-rat-race

Fontinelle, A. (2022, July 19). *Buying Private Health Insurance*. Investopedia. https://www.investopedia.com/articles/pf/08/private-health-insurance.asp

Gambhir, N. (2022, March 15). *What Is Life Insurance and How Does It Work? - Policygenius*. Policygenius. https://www.policygenius.com/life-insurance/how-does-life-insurance-work/?utm_source=google&utm_campaign=c:sem%7Cp:google%7Cv:life%7Cb:nb%7Cd:dt%7Ca:all%7Ci:all%7Cm:dsa&utm_medium=cpc&utm_content=506868216629&utm_term=&utm_location=1022762&utm_device=c&campaign_id=12560016618&lptest=&lptext=&gclid=CjwKCAjwgr6TBhAGEiwA3aVuITdoIIZ4DDpDcp5Yd-hu7KK5t_epjiWDluPrIZnQ3wP-gmKAsONvyAxoCFo0QAvD_BwE

Gobler, E. (2021, December 7). *The Best Trade Schools in New York | Become with*

REFERENCES

Lantern. LearnHowToBecome.org. https://www.learnhowtobe-come.org/trade-schools-new-york/#:~:text=Average%20Cost%20of%20-Trade%20School%20in%20New%20York&text=The%20average%20-cost%20of%20trade,below%2C%20not%20one%20exceeds%20%2430%2C000.

Gorton, D. (2022, June). *Understanding Taxes.* Investopedia. https://www.in-vestopedia.com/terms/t/taxes.asp#:~:text=27-,Why%20Do%20We%20-Pay%20Taxes%3F,emergency%20services%2C%20and%20welfare%20programs.

Gorton, D. (2022, June 27). *Understanding Taxes.* Investopedia. https://www.investopedia.com/terms/t/taxes.asp#toc-types-of-taxes

Hanks, C. (2018, January 31). *What is a Side Hustle? Meaning of a Side Gig & More - Wonolo.* Wonolo. https://www.wonolo.com/blog/what-is-a-side-hustle/

Hanson, M. (2021, December 27). *Average Cost of Community College [2022]: Tuition + Fees.* Education Data Initiative. https://educationda-ta.org/average-cost-of-community-college

Hodges, W. (2020, March 2). *Is Pet Insurance Worth It in 2022? Here's A Vet's Perspective.* Pawlicy Advisor; Pawlicy Advisor. https://www.pawlicy.-com/blog/is-pet-insurance-worth-it/

Holzhauer, B. (2021, September 3). *Here are the 5 states that don't have sales tax, and what you need to know about each.* CNBC; CNBC. https://www.cnbc.-com/select/states-with-no-sales-tax/

Horizon Farm Credit. (2020, September 1). *26 Factors Determining your Interest Rate | Horizon Farm Credit.* Horizonfc.com. https://www.horizonfc.-com/about/events/26-factors-determining-your-interest-rate-0

Horymski, C. (2022, April 29). *Consumer Debt Continued to Grow in 2021 Amid Economic Uncertainty.* Experian.com; Experian. https://www.experian.-com/blogs/ask-experian/research/consumer-debt-study/#:~:text=house-hold%20credit%20categories.-,Overall%20Debt%20Levels%20In-creased%205.4%25,increase%20from%202019%20through%202020.

Huffman, L., & Geller, E. (2020, December 17). *Is Travel Insurance Worth It?* NerdWallet. https://www.nerdwallet.com/article/travel/is-travel-insurance-worth-getting

Indeed Editorial. (2022, March 11). *50 Ways To Earn Passive Income as a College Student.* Indeed Career Guide. https://www.indeed.com/career-advice/finding-a-job/passive-income-college-students

Investopedia Team. (2021, April 9). *Credit History.* Investopedia. https://www.investopedia.com/terms/c/credit-history.asp

Investopedia Team. (2021, September 2). *What You Need to Know About Bankruptcy.* Investopedia. https://www.investopedia.com/articles/pf/07/bankruptcy.asp

Investopedia Team. (2022). *Homeowners Insurance Guide: A Beginner's Overview.* Investopedia. https://www.investopedia.com/insurance/homeowners-insurance-guide/

REFERENCES

Iowa State University. (2019, March). *Unit Pricing - Spend Smart Eat Smart.* Spend Smart Eat Smart. https://spendsmart.extension.iastate.edu/shop/compare-unit-prices-best-buy/

Irby, L. (2021, October 25). *How to Manage Your Debt.* The Balance. https://www.thebalance.com/how-to-manage-your-debt-960856

Irby, L. (2022, January 17). *A Quick Guide to Using Your Emergency Fund.* The Balance. https://www.thebalance.com/when-should-you-use-your-emergency-fund-453900

Jayakumar, A. (2019, June 6). *What Is a Loan?* NerdWallet. https://www.nerdwallet.com/article/loans/personal-loans/what-is-a-loan

Kagan, J. (2021, April 19). *Loan.* Investopedia. https://www.investopedia.com/terms/l/loan.asp

Kagan, J. (2022, July 18). *What Is Insurance?* Investopedia. https://www.investopedia.com/terms/i/insurance.asp

Kasasa. (2022). *Kasasa.* Kasasa.com. https://www.kasasa.com/blog/budgeting/common-budgeting-mistakes

Kungu, E. (2018, May 9). *Differences Between Assets and Liabilities | Difference Between.* Differencebetween.net. http://www.differencebetween.net/business/differences-between-assets-and-liabilities/

Kunsman, T. (2021, July 7). *Why You Need Multiple Streams of Income Starting Right Now.* Invested Wallet. https://investedwallet.com/multiple-streams-of-income/#:~:text=Creating%20multiple%20income%20streams%20allows,have%20something%20to%20fallback%20on.

Landes, C. (2021, June 2). *The Cost of Being Poor: Why It Costs So Much to Be Poor in America.* FinMasters. https://finmasters.com/cost-of-being-poor/#:~:text=It%27s%20expensive%20to%20be%20poor,poverty%20that%27s%20difficult%20to%20break.

Landicho, E. (2022, February 5). *Easy Passive Income Ideas for College Students in 2022.* Career Karma. https://careerkarma.com/blog/passive-income-for-college-students/

Lazarony, L. (2019, July 30). *How Interest Rates Work.* Credit.com. https://www.credit.com/personal-finance/how-interest-rates-work/#:~:text=In%20the%20case%20of%20money,P%20(1%20%2B%20rt).

Lisa, A. (2021, September 6). *23 Lottery Winners Who Lost Millions.* Yahoo.com. https://finance.yahoo.com/news/23-lottery-winners-lost-millions-190014709.html?guccounter=1&guce_referrer=aHR0cHM6Ly93d3cuZ29vZ2xlLmNvbS8&guce_referrer_sig=AQAAAKyuEw3K6pVQu2klJnfS0ghMdJOJPNWUubQ_osU1HaKDbnA0QjAB_06t66EAm3b_5yY01CxZrbADihvgaXa9nSam-7CW9k4mI5LLQKl_IsvM1xxz2AETdDG5uTTpJCvT-2XTsZ6AJs-V0GizrMjFutKLl1ULigxnNnaWoP2ZzWbK#:~:text=William%20Post,was%20%241%20million%20in%20debt.

Lusk, V. (2022, June 29). *The pros and cons of personal loans.* Bankrate;

REFERENCES

Bankrate.com. https://www.bankrate.com/loans/personal-loans/pros-cons-of-personal-loans/

Martins, A. (2022, March 23). *How Does Car Insurance Work?* Investopedia. https://www.investopedia.com/how-does-car-insurance-work-5180011

Maurer, C. (2020, June 23). *7 Reasons to Choose Quality over Quantity - #lessbutluxe*. #Lessbutluxe. https://lessbutluxe.com/quality-over-quantity/

Miczulski, M. (2018, April 2). *7 Ways to Save Money Shopping Online (Every Single Time)*. FinanceBuzz; FinanceBuzz. https://financebuzz.com/how-to-save-money-shopping-online

Miller, D. (2021, July 3). *Building credit history: Adding your kids as authorized users to your credit cards*. The Points Guy; https://thepointsguy.com/guide/children-authorized-users-credit-cards/

Nationwide. (2022). *Credit Card Tips and Advice – Nationwide*. Nationwide.com. https://www.nationwide.com/lc/resources/personal-finance/articles/guide-to-using-credit-card

Nowacki, L. (2022, February 18). *How To Set Up An Emergency Budget*. Rocket HQ; Rocket HQ. https://www.rockethq.com/learn/personal-finances/emergency-budget#:~:text=Unlike%20your%20normal%20daily%2C%20weekly,money%20further%20to%20last%20longer.

O'Connell, B. (2019, January 15). *What Are the Different Types of Interest and Why Do They Matter?* TheStreet; TheStreet. https://www.thestreet.com/personal-finance/education/different-types-of-interest-14833335

Parker, T. (2021, November 12). *When Are Personal Loans a Good Idea?* Investopedia. https://www.investopedia.com/articles/personal-finance/111715/when-are-personal-loans-good-idea.asp

Petrov, C. (2020, October 11). *20+ Incredible Personal Finance Statistics to Know in 2021*. SpendMeNot. https://spendmenot.com/blog/personal-finance-statistics/#:~:text=Around%2040%25%20of%20Americans%20have,by%20the%20Covid%2D19%20pandemic

Picchi, A. (2019, January 29). *40% of Americans only one missed paycheck away from poverty*. Cbsnews.com; CBS News. https://www.cbsnews.com/news/40-of-americans-one-step-from-poverty-if-they-miss-a-paycheck/

Point Editorial. (2021, December 8). *Advantages & Disadvantages of Banks: A Brief Overview*. Point.app; Point. https://www.point.app/article/advantages-disadvantages-of-banks-a-brief-overview

Porter, T. (2022, January 15). *8 low-risk ways to earn higher interest*. Bankrate; Bankrate.com. https://www.bankrate.com/banking/savings/low-risk-ways-to-earn-higher-interest/

Probasco, J. (2022, January 12). *Beyond Social Security and Medicare*. Investopedia. https://www.investopedia.com/special-government-help-for-your-retirement-5069756

Probasco, J. (2022, April 25). *How Much Money Do I Need to Retire?*

Investopedia. https://www.investopedia.com/retirement/how-much-you-should-have-saved-age/#toc-what-is-the-4-rule

Probasco, J. (2022, July 19). *9 States With No Income Tax*. Investopedia. https://www.investopedia.com/financial-edge/0210/7-states-with-no-income-tax.aspx

Pyles, S. (2018, July 2). *Good Debt vs. Bad Debt: Know the Difference*. NerdWallet. https://www.nerdwallet.com/article/finance/good-debt-vs-bad-debt

Ramsey Solutions. (2021, February 15). *Who Needs Long-Term Care Insurance?* Ramsey Solutions; Ramsey Solutions. https://www.ramseysolutions.com/insurance/who-needs-long-term-care-insurance

Ramsey Solutions. (2021, October 15). *Cash vs. Credit Card: Which Should I Use?* Ramsey Solutions; Ramsey Solutions. https://www.ramseysolutions.com/debt/cash-vs-credit-card

Resendiz, J. (2017, December 7). *How Credit Card Companies Make and Earn Money*. ValuePenguin; https://www.valuepenguin.com/how-do-credit-card-companies-make-money

Roosa. (2022, June 11). *Why Isn't Personal Finance Taught in School? - Money Marshmallow*. Money Marshmallow. https://moneymarshmallow.com/why-isnt-personal-finance-taught-in-school/

Ryan. (2021, May 17). *4 Simple Ways to Downsize your Life and Save Money in a Pinch*. APR Finder. https://www.aprfinder.com/4-simple-ways-downsize-life-save-money

Schlichter, S. (2022, February). *How Renters Insurance Works*. NerdWallet. https://www.nerdwallet.com/article/insurance/how-does-renters-insurance-work

Schlichter, S. (2022, July 1). *Is Pet Insurance Worth the Cost?* NerdWallet. https://www.nerdwallet.com/article/insurance/is-pet-insurance-worth-it

Scholarships.com. (2022). *The Pros And Cons Of Community Colleges - Scholarships.com*. Scholarships.com. https://www.scholarships.com/resources/college-prep/choosing-the-right-school/the-pros-and-cons-of-community-colleges/

Schwahn, L. (2020, December 18). *What Is a Budget?* NerdWallet. https://www.nerdwallet.com/article/finance/what-is-a-budget

Simmons, L. (2021, November 10). *The Pros and Cons of Trade School | BestColleges*. BestColleges.com. https://www.bestcolleges.com/resources/career-training/pros-and-cons-trade-school/#:~:text=Cons%20of%20trade%20school%20can,%2C%20financial%20aid%2C%20and%20flexibility.

Smith, L. (2021, April 29). *Good Debt vs. Bad Debt: What's the Difference?* Investopedia. https://www.investopedia.com/articles/pf/12/good-debt-bad-debt.asp

REFERENCES

SoFi. (2022, July 21). *39 Ways to Make Passive Income in 2022*. SoFi; SoFi. https://www.sofi.com/learn/content/how-to-manage-passive-income-streams/

Stanford University Vaden Health Services. (2021). *How U.S. Health Insurance Works* Vaden Health Services; Stanford University. https://vaden.stanford.edu/insurance-referral-office/health-insurance-overview/how-us-health-insurance-works#:~:text=Health%20insurance%20offers%20a%20way,who%20are%20making%20similar%20payments

Tax Foundation. (2018). *The Three Basic Tax Types | TaxEDU*. Tax Foundation. https://taxfoundation.org/the-three-basic-tax-types/

TD Bank. (2022). *How to Build a Good Credit Score and Credit History | TD Bank*. Td.com. https://www.td.com/us/en/personal-banking/finance/building-good-credit-score

Tech Times. (2017, January 17). *How To Shop Smart: 5 Characteristics Of A Smart Shopper*. Tech Times. https://www.techtimes.com/packsize/193131/20170117/how-to-shop-smart-5-characteristics-of-a-smart-shopper.htm

The Pretty Planeteer. (2021, January 22). *Cost Per Wear: How to Calculate The True Cost of Your Clothes*. Theprettyplaneteer.com. https://theprettyplaneteer.com/cost-per-wear-the-true-cost-of-your-clothes/

TransUnion. (2021, April 18). *Paying the Balance vs. Paying the Minimum on a Credit Card*. Transunion.com. https://www.transunion.com/blog/debt-management/credit-card-101-paying-the-balance-vs-paying-the-minimum

Tretina, K. (2022, April 25). *How to Get a Student Credit Card*. Investopedia. https://www.investopedia.com/how-to-get-a-student-credit-card-5191330

Tsosie, C. (2021, July 14). *What Happens If I Make Only the Minimum Payment on My Credit Card?* NerdWallet. https://www.nerdwallet.com/article/credit-cards/minimum-payment-credit-card

University of The People. (2020, July 27). *College Is A Scam: The Truth Behind The Tales*. University of the People; uopeople. https://www.uopeople.edu/blog/college-is-a-scam/

Washington Trust Bank. (2022). *The pros and cons of a side hustle*. Washington Trust Bank. https://www.watrust.com/resources/articles/career/the-pros-and-cons-of-a-side-hustle/#:~:text=A%20side%20hustle%20that%20becomes,it%2C%20and%20stick%20to%20them

WebMD. (2013, May 15). *How Health Care Reform Affects Employer Plans*. WebMD; https://www.webmd.com/health-insurance/health-insurance-coverage-through-employer

Wells, L. (2021, July 26). *CD vs. saving account: Which should you choose?* Bankrate; Bankrate.com. https://www.bankrate.com/banking/cd-vs-

savings/#:~:text=A%20CD%20is%20a%20low,better%20-
for%20medium%2Dterm%20goals

Western & Southern Financials Group. (2021, November 17). *5 Reasons to Start Preparing for Retirement Now*. Westernsouthern.com; Western & Southern Financial Group. https://www.westernsouthern.-com/learn/financial-education/5-reasons-to-start-preparing-for-retirement-now

Whiteside, E. (2022, March 5). *What Is the 50/20/30 Budget Rule?* Investopedia. https://www.investopedia.com/ask/answers/022916/what-502030-budget-rule.asp

Made in the USA
Columbia, SC
20 December 2022

74691257R00098